MATTHEW KENNEY'S
# BIG CITY COOKING

# MATTHEW KENNEY'S

# BIG

# COOK

# CITY ING

**RECIPES FOR A FAST-PACED WORLD**

BY MATTHEW KENNEY AND JOAN SCHWARTZ
PHOTOGRAPHS BY WILLIAM MEPPEM

CHRONICLE BOOKS
SAN FRANCISCO

TEXT COPYRIGHT © 2003 BY MATTHEW KENNEY.
PHOTOGRAPHS COPYRIGHT © 2003 BY WILLIAM MEPPEM.
ALL RIGHTS RESERVED. NO PART OF THIS BOOK MAY BE
REPRODUCED IN ANY FORM WITHOUT WRITTEN PERMISSION
FROM THE PUBLISHER.

LIBRARY OF CONGRESS CATALOGING-IN-PUBLICATION DATA
AVAILABLE.

ISBN 0-8118-3222-8

MANUFACTURED IN CHINA

PROP AND FOOD BY ALISON ATTENBOROUGH
DESIGNED BY SARA SCHNEIDER
TYPESETTING BY KRISTEN WURZ

DISTRIBUTED IN CANADA BY RAINCOAST BOOKS
9050 SHAUGHNESSY STREET
VANCOUVER, BC V6P 6E5

10 9 8 7 6 5 4 3 2 1

CHRONICLE BOOKS LLC
85 SECOND STREET
SAN FRANCISCO, CALIFORNIA 94105

WWW.CHRONICLEBOOKS.COM

## DEDICATION

To Sarma Melngailis.
—M. K.

To my family: Allen, David, Rachel, and Deborah—and welcome to John—with love.
—J. S.

## ACKNOWLEDGMENTS

It takes a big city to make a book.  I would like to thank:

My agent, Jane Dystel; editor, Bill LeBlond; coauthor, Joan Schwartz.

Josh Capon, Sarah Wilson, Christopher Robins, Jon LoPreisti, Jenny Glasgow, Ernesto Barbosa, Larry Kolar, Jeffrey Slade, and Alex Espiritu, for their culinary passion and expertise.

Christian Palicuka, Chris Spann, Michael Glick, Sam Governale, and Jean Marc Neyret for their leadership in our dining rooms.

Olivier Cheng and Bettina Klinger for their vision.

Boyd Willat, Govantez Lowndes, and Rasim Ozkanca for their continued support and inspiration.

Sandrine Lago, Deana Fumando, Derek Nettles, Mark Wood, and the team at the Matthew Kenney Group.

Robert, Shirley, and Patrick Kenney; and Maryellen and Paul Schoeman.

The entire staff at all of our restaurants for their dedication.

Special thanks to my partner in business and life, Sarma Melngailis, for her limitless contributions to this book and its recipes, which have influenced the way in which I look at food and cooking today.

# TABLE OF CONTENTS

Chicken Glazed with Honey, Lime, and Chile  78

Duck Breast with Pomegranate Baste  79

Spicy Soy-Glazed Beef Filet with Shiitakes and Bok Choy  80

Pan-Crisped Goat Cheese with Figs and Arugula  81

Pineapple and Rhubarb with Brown Sugar and Basil  83

Caramelized Mango with Lime and Blueberries  84

Cherries Sautéed in Pinot Noir with Crème Fraîche  85

## 4/ FROM THE TERRACE

Lime and Honey Glazed Eggplant with Mint Chutney  90

Charred Vegetables with Orange Blossom Honey and Pecorino  92

Red Chile Barbecued Salmon with Coconut Basmati Rice  93

Grilled Swordfish with Green Olive Tapenade  94

Miso-Grilled Tuna with Savoy Cabbage  95

Moroccan Spiced Shrimp with Artichokes and Pomegranate  96

Brochette of Lamb with Honey-Lime Marinade  98

Rosemary-Grilled Venison with Grilled Peaches  99

Maple-Balsamic Glazed Pork Chops with Pecans and Ginger  101

Grilled Figs with Lemon Ricotta and Rosemary Syrup  102

Bittersweet Chocolate Bruschetta  104

## 5/ ROASTING FAST AND SLOW

Warm Goat Cheese Tarts with Fig Jam and Rosemary  110

Parmigiano-Reggiano Pudding  112

BLT Pizza  113

Wild Mushroom Pizza  114

Truffled Macaroni and Cheese  116

Baked Pasta with Zucchini and Asiago  117

Halibut Baked in Parchment with Tomatoes, Lime, and Cilantro  119

Slow-Roasted Salmon with Yogurt and Cardamom  120

Salt-Baked Salmon  121

Cheddar Meatloaf  122

Roast Chicken with Lemon, Sage, and Pine Nuts  123

Roasted Lamb Loin Stuffed with Almonds, Dates, Goat Cheese, and Mint  124

Coriander-Crusted Pork Loin Stuffed with Dried Peaches and Pine Nuts  126

Chocolate Ganache Cake with Whipped Cream  128

# PREFACE

Living in a large city can be challenging for food lovers. I know this firsthand, having spent years trying to balance a busy lifestyle with my passion for cooking and eating at home. For many of us, our careers seem to demand a growing majority of our time. Our kitchens are often small and occasionally resemble moderate-sized closets, containing no room for equipment, large quantities of supplies, or movement. Quality products, while abundant, are often available only in crowded gourmet markets and require a good amount of navigation to find. Still, those of us who value great food will go to great lengths to find a way to make each meal count. Once we learn to use the limitations of the city to our advantage, it actually becomes easy to organize our lives and our kitchens in a way that allows us to enjoy food the way we prefer. The recipes in this book reflect this philosophy and share a common sensibility. They are up-to-date, clean, and, most important, they can all be prepared within a busy lifestyle or in a small kitchen with limited equipment.

The cooking I like today is the product of many influences, including childhood experiences, restaurants where I have worked and the cooks in those restaurants, extensive travel, personal tastes, and the best foods in my favorite markets. To this day, I am deeply influenced by the clean, exotic flavors that I first experienced in the kitchen at Malvasia, owned by Chef Gennaro Piccone. His use of citrus, herbs, and seasonal produce, and his light-handed style, began the formation of the type of cuisine I now love. Travels throughout the Mediterranean, including Morocco, Egypt, Sicily, Turkey, and Spain, have given me tastes of the best products of those regions. Nuts and spices from the markets of Marrakesh, fresh baby shrimp in Malaga, dates in Istanbul, and wild fennel pasta in Palermo all added to my taste sensibility and mental library, as I like to think of it. Perhaps the most important contribution to this style comes from the time I have spent on the coast of Maine, both growing up and today. It was there that I began my close relationship to nature and its products. Once you have tasted just-picked peas in early summer or wild blueberries in August, you begin to realize that the quality of ingredients is everything in cooking, and that it is often better to do little other than support them. Of course, the way I cook is also dictated by my lifestyle, rather small kitchen, and limited storage space, and by the way I feel when I eat full-flavored yet clean and light foods.

*Big City Cooking* is really a lifestyle food book as much as it is a cookbook. For this reason, I have focused a good amount of attention on finding the right ingredients, storing them, and creating recipes that will not turn your kitchen upside down. The chapters are organized by cooking method rather than by food category, to address the needs of the home cook. For example, "Chapter 2: Simply Raw to Barely Cooked," contains recipes that are colorful, light, and often easy to prepare. These dishes are ideal for a warm summer night and a kitchen with limited or no cooking equipment available. Many can be prepared with just a sharp knife and a cutting board. Alternatively, "Chapter 6: Simmering Stews and Hot Pots," offers dishes that can make a meal for many using one burner and one cooking vessel. Most of these dishes can be made in advance and served family style, allowing you to spend time cooking before your guests arrive and to minimize your time away from them once they get there. This is the way I cook at home, making decisions based on the equipment and products available, where I am, and how much time I have to spend in the kitchen, which is usually not as much as I would like.

Throughout the book, I refer to the importance of quality ingredients, at their best in their peak season. To help you find and select the best ingredients, we have developed a Sources list, which includes some of the best Web sites for ordering hard-to-find products, as well as descriptions that will help you recognize top-quality ingredients. On many occasions, I have no idea what I am going to cook before I go to the market and find what looks best and what inspires me most. We all seem to have our favorite market, and I urge you to find your inspiration there. Try to familiarize yourself with the seasonality of ingredients, and buy what is in its prime at that time; big city markets have access to products that are in season all over the world. It makes the entire cooking process more enjoyable.

I love coming home with bags of incredibly fresh ingredients and looking at them, smelling them, and working with them. All of the recipes in this book are made with the thought of great ingredients in mind. It is just as important to spend time choosing the right ingredients as it is to choose what you will be cooking.

In one way or another, my restaurants all incorporate the philosophies of this book into their menus and concepts. They are in urban areas, and most of our guests expect ingredients of the highest quality prepared in a relatively simple way. We strive to find products that can be used in comfortable, up-to-date surroundings. Each restaurant provides a different experience, but all strictly adhere to the idea of showcasing the best products in an interesting yet straightforward manner. Many of the recipes in this book are on the different menus from time to time. For example, Commune revolves around the idea of sharing food and wine and works well for large groups. The menu has many dishes designed for sharing. It changes frequently, with the seasons, and strives to re-create the concept of a tavern for today's urban lifestyle. Among the recipes from Commune that you'll find here are Salt-Baked Salmon (page 121), a straightforward dish that we always serve with the freshest vegetables, and Crab Cakes with Lemony Rémoulade (page 74), a classic that we make with the best crabmeat from Maine.

Commissary, in Portland, Maine, is probably the best example of this style of cooking. Seared Scallops with Caramelized Cauliflower and Brown Butter Vinaigrette (page 70) and Warm Goat Cheese Tarts with Fig Jam and Rosemary (page 110) are two of my favorite dishes that were developed at Commissary, using the best ingredients available. Our newest restaurant, Commissary NY, takes this concept even further, with menus that vary each week. Several of the dishes in this book are from our opening menu, such as Roasted Lamb Loin Stuffed with Almonds, Dates, Goat

Cheese, and Mint (page 124). We serve it with the Saffron Fregula that, in this book, you will find paired with Lamb Stew with Pomegranate (page 160). Other popular dishes that have been on the Commissary NY menu include Seared Sea Bass with Anise, Pistachios, and Meyer Lemon Purée (page 75); and Arugula with Manchego, Roasted Almonds, and Quince Dressing (page 37). Throughout our company, from our pâtisserie, Sugar, to our catering company, every recipe is ingredient driven and strives to make use of the best of what is available and in season.

My favorite kitchen in which to prepare these dishes is at home. The recipes are part of a lifestyle built around the preparation and enjoyment of good food, and at the same time they recognize the day-to-day limitations on the time we are able to spend cooking and shopping. With proper planning and shopping, it is relatively easy to make each meal count.

—Matthew Kenney

**CHAPTER 1/**
**INGREDIENTS: URBAN HUNTING AND GATHERING**

# INGREDIENTS:   URBAN

It's a well-known fact that urbanites get the pick of the crop. All kinds of foods that don't make it to small-town markets are available in big cities, which offer easy access to top-quality baked goods, cheeses, condiments, exotic imports, and the latest, hottest ideas from innovative suppliers. This lush variety inspires you to be creative—a beautiful display of fish, poultry, or meat tempts you, or an unusual herb, vegetable, or grain catches your eye, and you're on your way. Stores are easy to reach, and although they may be crowded, they are entertaining (many a fine conversation has ripened on a long checkout line).

Some cities have spectacular year-round greenmarkets that offer the best seasonal local produce, but your food shopping needn't be limited by the season. It is always summer somewhere in the world, and merchants display beautiful produce flown in at the peak of freshness, any time of year. The world is the city shopper's garden—and if there happens to be something you can't find locally for that special meal you are planning, you can order it in a click from a Web site.

Amid this plenty, how do you choose? Here are a few commonsense tips to ensure that you always buy the best.

Experience has taught me that the most important thing you can do as a shopper is to find a market (or markets) that you like and establish yourself as a regular customer. Get to know the staff, the layout, and the specialties. You will learn where to look for the specific foods you want and thus cut down your shopping time. As a frequent visitor, you will be able to recognize what has just come in, what is good, and what is better passed by. The people who work there will recognize and cater to you.

For example, I love Meyer lemons. They are sweeter and less acidic than regular lemons, and I enjoy fitting them into existing recipes, such as vinaigrettes, or creating new recipes around them (see, for example, Seared Sea Bass with Anise, Pistachio, and Meyer Lemon Purée, page 75). Every year, as winter winds down and

# HUNTING AND GATHERING

spring approaches, I track their arrival at my favorite market. The produce manager alerts me when they are expected so I can get first crack at the shipment; and when new cartons are unloaded, I can distinguish the fresh additions to the bin from the ones that have been sitting around for a while. There are subtle differences in the fruit as the season progresses, and I'm not surprised when later lemons are a little weaker than those I bought at their peak. My friend at the market also lets me know when the deliveries will be ending, so I can stock up.

When you shop for vegetables and fruits, make sure they are shiny with color, vibrant, and crisp—paleness is an indication that they are no longer fresh. A perfectly ripe specimen will feel heavy and appear to be full of water, which is its life source. If it looks dry or drained, or if its leaves have started to turn yellow, pass it by. Beware of giant asparagus, carrots, or zucchini—they are overgrown and past their prime in flavor and texture. As with the Meyer lemons, notice when fresh shipments arrive. And it's not a bad idea to make your choice from the back of the heap, where the newest fruits and vegetables are usually placed.

In shopping for seafood, again, it helps to develop a relationship with one market, where you will be sure to get the freshest products. Fresh fish should be translucent, shiny, firm, and springy to the touch. It should have a subtle aroma of the sea—never a fishy smell. Even small fish markets can provide that quality, but unfortunately, it seems that many purveyors want to sell what they've had the longest, so you must know what you are looking for.

Find a meat market whose quality you trust. Take notes over time, so you can remember what meats you have bought and liked. And follow the clues of the neighborhood, being aware that butchers in certain localities will pay special attention to the cuts that are most popular with their customers. On Manhattan's Upper East Side, for example, you can expect butchers to have more experience with tenderloins and filets, while in some other areas, meat for braising or stews may be more available.

Buy the freshest nuts and seeds you can find, from a store that has a high turnover. When a recipe calls for toasted nuts or seeds, you can toast them in a skillet over medium heat for about 4 minutes, shaking the skillet often, or place them in a 325°F oven for 4 to 7 minutes (seeds will take less time than nuts). In both methods, watch carefully to make sure they do not burn. I find that the flavor is greatly enhanced if you toast them with a small amount of salt and a little oil to help the salt adhere (use nut oil, if you have some). Toasted nuts and seeds will generally keep for up to 2 weeks in an airtight container in the refrigerator and can be a great addition to a variety of foods, from salads and pastas to meats, fish, and desserts.

Purchase whole spices when you can, and grind them fresh for each use in a spice grinder or a small coffee grinder reserved for spices only. Buy whole nutmeg and grate it yourself—you will find it to be infinitely better than commercially packaged ground nutmeg. Although most of my recipes call for kosher salt, feel free to substitute either coarse sea salt or fleur de sel—a fantastic French sea salt that is harvested by hand. Of course, kosher salt, the least expensive and most easily available of the three, is the choice when you are cooking grains or pasta, but fleur de sel and coarse sea salt are excellent sprinkled on meats or fish, because you can see and taste the individual grains and feel their texture. Be careful not to overseason with these salts; the grains may not dissolve immediately, making it easy to add more than you need. Recipes for cakes and other desserts simply call for "salt," meaning the familiar table variety.

I love the pungence, fruity aroma, and flavor of really good olive oil, and I urge you to buy the best you can find, preferably extra-virgin. If I had to pick a favorite, it would be Italian oil, but the Moroccan and Greek varieties, which are a little stronger in flavor, are excellent, too. I cook with extra-virgin olive oil, and I suggest it in my recipes. It adds deep flavor to a dish, and it has a light, fresh feel on the palate. Its burning point is lower than that of some other oils, but the recipes in this book are somewhat delicate and don't require cooking at extremely high heat. You may choose to cook with plain olive oil, but be sure to use extra-virgin for all vinaigrettes and for drizzling over food.

A special boon for big city shoppers is the large number of excellent gourmet markets—my favorite is just across the street from my apartment. You may have to pay more at these markets than you would in a supermarket, but I strongly believe that better-quality food is always worth the price. And finally, take advantage of the city's wealth of ethnic shops for all sorts of specialty spices, fruits, vegetables, seafood, and meats.

### A WORD ABOUT CONDIMENTS

Many of my dishes contain recipes for vinaigrettes, sauces, or condiments such as lemony rémoulade, tomato jam, green olive tapenade, quince dressing, balsamic syrup, and Meyer lemon purée. When you find one that you especially like, feel free to use it as a garnish, as a substitute in other recipes, or in your own creations. Or vary some of the sauces and garnishes in this book with different main ingredients. For example, try the ginger dressing (from Seared Tuna with Ginger Dressing, page 76) with chicken, shellfish, or beef—or toss it with fresh greens. Try spooning the mint chutney (from Lime and Honey Glazed Eggplant with Mint Chutney, page 90) over grilled lamb chops. Always cook with an eye toward creativity.

# BIG CITY, SMALL KITCHEN

The first word that comes to mind when people think of a city kitchen is "tiny," although you may prefer the terms "compact" or "space challenged." But a lot of good meals can come out of a small workplace, if it is well organized and used efficiently. Some of the finest restaurants prove this daily.

You can make the most of your kitchen, whatever its size. If workspace is limited, don't park your small appliances, such as coffeemakers or toasters, on the counter. They clutter the surfaces and make things look generally messy. Hang pots and pans, as well as kitchen tools, from wall hooks. And cut down on the number of gadgets you collect—if you haven't used something for a month or two, consider getting rid of it. The goal should be to have as much clear working space as possible.

Your food storage space is probably limited as well, so maximize it whenever you can. Transfer ingredients to easy-to-use containers, preferably well-designed receptacles that stack on top of one another. Put your ground spices in tins or shakers that take up little space in your cupboard. Make your containers functional: When you buy a bottle of olive oil, attach a pouring spout to it; then, when you need the oil, you can just pour it out. Virtually every ingredient can be transferred into something that is easier to use than the package it came in. Instead of carelessly stowing ingredients in the cupboard, organize them by food categories. That way you will always know where they are and you won't have to search when you start to cook. In one part of a cabinet, keep olive oil, vinegars, and honey; in another, spices, sugars, and flours. This is the way a restaurant kitchen is set up—everything makes sense. In your refrigerator, keep butter, cheeses, and yogurts in one area. Separate meats from fish and fruits from vegetables. Compartmentalization always makes it easier to find things—you cut down on your movement and use up a lot less space than you would if things were randomly put away.

Whenever possible, buy in small amounts rather than large. You don't want to take up space unnecessarily, and in the city, you are close enough to stores to shop often and spontaneously. (Spontaneity also makes the cooking process a lot more fun.) Keep everything accessible, clean, and fresh. Rotate your stock periodically—move the oldest goods to the front, and dump anything that is past its prime.

Make your style of cooking, serving, and cleanup as efficient as possible, and remember that cleaning up as you work is critical. Take a few minutes between tasks to scrub your pots and pans and to put bowls and tools into the dishwasher. Preparing recipes is easier when you're not elbowing sticky implements out of your way and dealing with clutter. And it's certainly more enjoyable to finish your meal and not have to spend your downtime straightening up a messy kitchen, even a small one.

# YOUR KITCHEN TOOL CHEST

Here is a list of all the equipment called for in our recipes—you'll find it is a good basis for an efficient and pared-down kitchen. But you can finesse it a bit, as space requires. You can make do with a minimum of pots and pans, rewashing and reusing one or two in the course of preparing a meal. You may choose to do without a pizza stone or to pound your meat with the flat bottom of a glass bottle if you don't have a mallet. You may decide to forgo a large roasting pan (often a large sauté pan will do), a blender or mortar and pestle (if you find a processor more versatile), and a toaster oven (if your stove has an oven-broiler). You can make sure that all your mixing bowls are nonreactive rather than keeping a double set, and call cups and soup bowls into service to replace small mixing bowls. But everything you own should be of good quality and, whenever possible, attractive as well—your nicest bowls, pots, and pans are naturals for serving.

## TOOL CHEST

BAKING PANS:
  8- OR 9-INCH SQUARE CAKE PAN
  8- OR 9-INCH ROUND CAKE PAN
  9-BY-13-INCH GLASS OR CERAMIC BAKING DISH
  LOAF PAN
  ROASTING PAN
  BAKING SHEETS (2)
BLENDER
BRUSHES: A STIFF WIRE BRUSH FOR GRILL CLEANING;
  SOFT PASTRY BRUSHES (LONG AND SHORT) FOR
  GLAZING GRILLED FOODS
COLANDER
CONTAINERS, PREFERABLY STACKING, FOR PANTRY
  STORAGE
ELECTRIC MIXER
FOOD PROCESSOR OR MINIPROCESSOR
GRATER (PREFERABLY MICROPLANE)
GRILL (CHARCOAL OR GAS)
KNIVES, ALL VERY SHARP, INCLUDING A LONG, THIN
  NONSERRATED KNIFE; A SMALL PARING KNIFE; AND
  A CHEF'S KNIFE
LADLE
MALLET, FOR POUNDING MEAT
MANDOLINE: USEFUL FOR THIN-SLICING VEGETABLES.
  THE PLASTIC ONES ARE FINE; THEY ARE MUCH
  CHEAPER THAN THE TRADITIONAL METAL MODELS
  AND ARE EASIER TO WORK WITH AND KEEP CLEAN.
MEASURING CUPS
MEASURING SPOONS
MIXING BOWLS: LARGE, MEDIUM, AND SMALL
  (PREFERABLY NONREACTIVE)

MORTAR AND PESTLE
PARCHMENT PAPER
PEPPER MILL
PIZZA STONE (BAKING STONE)
PLATTERS, FOR SERVING
POTS, SAUCEPANS: SMALL, MEDIUM, LARGE,
  EXTRA LARGE; ALL HEAVY DUTY WITH LIDS
RAMEKINS: 6 INDIVIDUAL CERAMIC (6-OUNCE)
SAUTÉ PANS: LARGE STRAIGHT SIDED
SHEARS OR SCISSORS, KITCHEN
SKEWERS, WOODEN OR METAL
SKILLETS (FRYING PANS): SMALL, MEDIUM, LARGE;
  MEDIUM NONSTICK; ALL WITH LIDS AND PREFERABLY
  WITH OVENPROOF HANDLES; MEDIUM CAST-IRON PAN;
  GRILL PAN
SPATULA, METAL
SPATULA, RUBBER
SPICE GRINDER (USE A SMALL COFFEE GRINDER)
SPOON, SLOTTED
SPOONS, WOODEN
STRAINERS, FINE AND COARSE
STRING OR TWINE
TOASTER OVEN
TONGS, LONG AND SHORT
TOWELS, HEAVY-DUTY KITCHEN (GOOD FOR GRABBING
  HOT POTS AND PANS)
WHISK, MEDIUM
ZESTER OR VEGETABLE PEELER

# YOUR PANTRY

Of course, your shelves will be stocked with the basics: salt, peppercorns, white and brown sugar, and all-purpose flour; and your refrigerator will have milk, butter, eggs, lemons, and limes. Here are a few equally useful ingredients called for in our recipes. You don't need to keep all of them in your larder all the time, but you should know where to find them when you need them.

Remember, a dish is only as good as what goes into it, so it is crucial that you select the best possible ingredients. Look at it this way: You have to shop, and in many cases an excellent purveyor is just down the street from that dull, clueless chain store. It's important to walk those few extra steps—or in some cases, to log on to a reliable Web site—if the effort gets you standout ingredients that will make your meal a success. For example, you can buy waxy, supermarket-brand Cheddar, or you can buy Grafton or Montgomery Cheddar and suddenly find yourself in a better universe. You can choose the same old bacon, or you can visit the Niman Ranch Web site and discover totally new flavor and quality. Most of the items listed here are easy to find in well-stocked markets, and they are all available online as well. Descriptions and Web sites are included.

## ON THE PANTRY SHELF

### ALMOND EXTRACT
Use in desserts. Look for superior-quality extract with natural flavor.
WWW.ADRIANASCARAVAN.COM
WWW.DIAMONDORGANICS.COM

### ALMOND FLOUR, TOASTED
Pulverized toasted almonds.
WWW.KINGARTHURFLOUR.COM
WWW.NUTS4U.COM

### AMARETTI, LAZZARONI BRAND
Crisp almond cookies.
WWW.CYBERCUCINA.COM
WWW.DITALIA.COM
WWW.ETHNICGROCER.COM

### BEANS, CANNELLINI
Dried small, white beans.
WWW.CHEFSHOP.COM
WWW.THEFOODSTORES.COM
WWW.GLOBALFOODMARKET.COM
WWW.SULTANSDELIGHT.COM
WWW.KALUSTYANS.COM

### CHOCOLATE
Use good quality, such as Callebaut, Scharffen Berger, or Valrhona for desserts.
WWW.CHOCOSPHERE.COM
WWW.ADRIANASCARAVAN.COM
WWW.BAKINGSHOP.COM
WWW.GLOBALFOODMARKET.COM
WWW.SCHARFFENBERGER.COM

### COUSCOUS
Couscous looks like a small grain but is made from coarsely ground durum wheat. As a side dish, it soaks up flavorful sauces.
WWW.ADRIANASCARAVAN.COM

WWW.CHEFSHOP.COM
WWW.CITARELLA.COM
WWW.DIAMONDORGANICS.COM
WWW.ETHNICGROCER.COM
WWW.GLOBALFOODMARKET.COM

### FARRO OR EMMER
A type of hulled wheat that is very low in gluten and nutritionally superior to ordinary wheat. It has a nutlike flavor and chewy texture.
WWW.CHEFSHOP.COM
WWW.CITARELLA.COM
WWW.CYBERCUCINA.COM
WWW.FARAWAYFOODS.COM
WWW.GLOBALFOODMARKET.COM
WWW.KALUSTYANS.COM

### FENNEL POLLEN
Yellow pollen from Tuscan wild fennel plants. Use to season chicken, fish, or pork before cooking.
WWW.ADRIANASCARAVAN.COM
WWW.CHEFSHOP.COM
WWW.DEANDELUCA.COM
WWW.ZINGERMANS.COM

### FLEUR DE SEL
Hand-harvested French sea salt. Many chefs consider it the best salt.
WWW.ADRIANASCARAVAN.COM
WWW.CHEFSHOP.COM
WWW.DEANDELUCA.COM

### FREGULA, FREGULA SARDA (MAY ALSO BE SPELLED "FREGOLA")
Toasted Italian grainlike pasta made from semolina. Nuttier and chewier than regular couscous. May be listed online as Italian couscous.
WWW.CYBERCUCINA.COM
WWW.GLOBALFOODMARKET.COM
WWW.PASTACO.COM

## FRUIT, DRIED

Provides concentrated fruit flavor; stores well.

WWW.CITARELLA.COM

WWW.DIAMONDORGANICS.COM

WWW.MELISSAS.COM

WWW.NUTS4U.COM

## GIANDUJA (MAY ALSO BE SPELLED "GIANDUIA")

A classic combination of chocolate and hazelnuts, available in blocks or individually wrapped pieces.

WWW.BAKINGSHOP.COM

WWW.CYBERCUCINA.COM

WWW.DAPRANO.COM

## GINGER, CANDIED OR CRYSTALIZED

Ginger that has been cooked in sugar syrup until it is candylike.

WWW.ADRIANASCARAVAN.COM

WWW.CHEFSHOP.COM

WWW.CITARELLA.COM

WWW.KINGARTHURFLOUR.COM

WWW.MELISSAS.COM

## HONEY, ORANGE BLOSSOM

Produced from the nectar of orange blossoms, this honey has a hint of orange flavor.

WWW.ASIAMEX.COM

WWW.CHEFSHOP.COM

WWW.THEFOODSTORES.COM

WWW.KALUSTYANS.COM

## HONEY, WHITE TRUFFLE

Made by Restaurant Lulu in San Francisco, this honey has the subtle flavor of white truffles.

WWW.ADRIANASCARAVAN.COM

WWW.CHEFSHOP.COM

WWW.FARAWAYFOODS.COM

WWW.RESTAURANTLULU.COM

## MIRIN

Sweet Japanese rice wine, used in cooking.

WWW.ADRIANASCARAVAN.COM

WWW.ASIAMEX.COM

WWW.ETHNICGROCER.COM

## NUTS

Almonds, hazelnuts, pine nuts, pistachios, walnuts. Look for almonds that have already been roasted and salted, to save a step.

WWW.CITARELLA.COM

WWW.NUTS4U.COM

WWW.PASTACO.COM

WWW.SULTANSDELIGHT.COM

## OIL, EXTRA-VIRGIN OLIVE

The first and purest pressing of olives, with low acid and fruity flavor.

WWW.CHEFSHOP.COM

WWW.CITARELLA.COM

WWW.CYBERCUCINA.COM

WWW.DEANDELUCA.COM

## OIL, NUT (ALMOND, HAZELNUT, WALNUT, AND OTHERS)

Oil pressed from nuts, used in vinaigrettes and for drizzling over food.

WWW.CHEFSHOP.COM

WWW.GLOBALFOODMARKET.COM

WWW.THEFOODSTORES.COM

## OIL, TRUFFLE

Olive oil flavored with truffles.

WWW.ADRIANASCARAVAN.COM

WWW.CITARELLA.COM

WWW.DEANDELUCA.COM

WWW.FARAWAYFOODS.COM

WWW.CYBERCUCINA.COM

## OLD BAY SEASONING

A traditional spice blend often used in crab cakes and other seafood preparations.
WWW.ADRIANASCARAVAN.COM
WWW.CITARELLA.COM

## PALM SUGAR

An unrefined sugar with a coconut-like flavor made from palm tree sap. It comes in both soft and solid form and can be found in East Indian markets.
WWW.ADRIANASCARAVAN.COM
WWW.CHEFSHOP.COM
WWW.GLOBALFOODMARKET.COM

## PANKO CRUMBS

Coarse, irregular-sized Japanese bread crumbs. Panko crumbs adhere to food, are easy to work with, produce beautifully crisp crusts, and keep well.
WWW.ADRIANASCARAVAN.COM
WWW.ETHNICGROCER.COM
WWW.GLOBALFOODMARKET.COM

## PASTA, FARRO

Pasta made from farro, a grain with a nutlike flavor. It is especially high in nutrients.
WWW.CHEFSHOP.COM
WWW.CYBERCUCINA.COM
WWW.DEANDELUCA.COM
WWW.GLOBALFOODMARKET.COM
WWW.MURRAYSCHEESE.COM

## PASTA, GARGANELLI

Tubular, ribbed pasta, similar to penne rigata.
WWW.FARAWAYFOODS.COM
WWW.ITALIANFOODS.COM

## PASTA, GEMELLI

Short pasta twists made from 2 strands of pasta.
WWW.DEANDELUCA.COM

## PASTA, WHOLE WHEAT

Pasta made from whole-wheat flour. Has an assertive, nutty flavor.
WWW.PASTACO.COM
WWW.WINECHEESE.COM

## POLENTA

Ground cornmeal used to make polenta, the dish that is a staple of northern and central Italy.
WWW.ADRIANASCARAVAN.COM
WWW.CHEFSHOP.COM
WWW.CYBERCUCINA.COM
WWW.FARAWAYFOODS.COM
WWW.GLOBALFOODMARKET.COM

## POMEGRANATE MOLASSES

Pomegranate juice reduced to a sweet syrup.
WWW.ADRIANASCARAVAN.COM
WWW.KALUSTYANS.COM
WWW.GLOBALFOODMARKET.COM
WWW.TURKISHTASTE.COM

## RICE, ARBORIO

A short-kernel, starchy rice used for risotto.
WWW.CHEFSHOP.COM
WWW.CYBERCUCINA.COM
WWW.DITALIA.COM
WWW.GLOBALFOODMARKET.COM
WWW.FARAWAYFOODS.COM
WWW.PASTACO.COM

## RICE, BASMATI

A fragrant Indian rice.
WWW.ADRIANASCARAVAN.COM
WWW.CITARELLA.COM
WWW.DIAMONDORGANICS.COM
WWW.ETHNICGROCER.COM
WWW.GLOBALFOODMARKET.COM
WWW.PASTACO.COM
WWW.SULTANSDELIGHT.COM

## SPICES, WHOLE AND GROUND:

(aniseed, cardamom, cloves, cumin seeds, juniper berries, saffron, star anise, and others) These aromatic flavorings are best used within 6 months of purchase. Grind your own for superior flavor.
WWW.ADRIANASCARAVAN.COM
WWW.DEANDELUCA.COM
WWW.ETHNICGROCER.COM
WWW.GLOBALFOODMARKET.COM
WWW.PENZEYS.COM

## TAPIOCA

Pearl-like pellets extracted from the cassava plant, used to thicken puddings and other desserts.
WWW.ASIAMEX.COM

## VANILLA BEANS; VANILLA EXTRACT

The aromatic, flavorful vanilla seeds come in a thin, dried pod; or substitute the pure natural—not artificial—extract.
WWW.ADRIANASCARAVAN.COM
WWW.CHEFSHOP.COM
WWW.KINGARTHURFLOUR.COM

## VINEGAR, AGED BALSAMIC

Full-flavored vinegar aged in barrels for several years.
WWW.ADRIANASCARAVAN.COM
WWW.CHEFSHOP.COM
WWW.CITARELLA.COM
WWW.DEANDELUCA.COM
WWW.FARAWAYFOODS.COM

## VINEGAR, FIG BALSAMIC

Balsamic vinegar flavored with figs.
WWW.ADRIANASCARAVAN.COM
WWW.GLOBALFOODMARKET.COM
WWW.RESTAURANTLULU.COM

## IN THE REFRIGERATOR: CHEESES AND BUTTER

## ASIAGO

Aged cow's milk cheese. Italian has a mild, sweet flavor and soft texture; Wisconsin has a mild, tangy flavor and harder texture.
WWW.IGOURMET.COM
WWW.MURRAYSCHEESE.COM
WWW.WORLDOFCHEESE.COM

## CHEDDAR

Cow's milk cheese with firm texture. Montgomery and Grafton are excellent varieties.
WWW.CITARELLA.COM
WWW.DEANDELUCA.COM
WWW.IGOURMET.COM
WWW.MURRAYSCHEESE.COM
WWW.WORLDOFCHEESE.COM

## FROMAGE BLANC

White, soft cheese made from milk curd, with little or no fat.
WWW.IGOURMET.COM

## GREAT HILL BLUE

Ripened blue cheese, made from raw cow's milk. Strongly flavored, award winning.
WWW.GREATHILLBLUE.COM
WWW.IGOURMET.COM
WWW.WINECHEESE.COM
WWW.WORLDOFCHEESE.COM

## MANCHEGO

Semifirm Spanish cheese with a mild, nutlike flavor. Milder (aged up to 2 months) is preferred.
WWW.DEANDELUCA.COM
WWW.IGOURMET.COM
WWW.MURRAYSCHEESE.COM
WWW.WINECHEESE.COM
WWW.WORLDOFCHEESE.COM

## MOZZARELLA, FRESH

Mild, soft white cow's (or buffalo's) milk cheese with sweet flavor, good melting quality.

WWW.DEANDELUCA.COM
WWW.IGOURMET.COM
WWW.MURRAYSCHEESE.COM
WWW.WINECHEESE.COM

## PARMIGIANO-REGGIANO

Hard cow's milk cheese with complex, nutty flavor, good for grating.

WWW.CITARELLA.COM
WWW.DEANDELUCA.COM
WWW.DITALIA.COM
WWW.ESPERYA.COM
WWW.IGOURMET.COM
WWW.MURRAYSCHEESE.COM
WWW.WINECHEESE.COM
WWW.WORLDOFCHEESE.COM

## PECORINO TOSCANO

Hard sheep's milk cheese with tangy flavor, good for grating.

WWW.IGOURMET.COM
WWW.MURRAYSCHEESE.COM
WWW.WORLDOFCHEESE.COM

## RICOTTA, FRESH

Light, delicate, and moist cheese made from the whey of cow's or sheep's milk.

WWW.IGOURMET.COM
WWW.MURRAYSCHEESE.COM

## TRUFFLE BUTTER

Truffle-flavored sweet butter.

WWW.DARTAGNAN.COM
WWW.GLOBALFOODMARKET.COM
WWW.IGOURMET.COM
WWW.URBANI.COM

## PRODUCE AND CONDIMENTS

### BLOOD ORANGES

Tart and sweet red-fleshed orange.

WWW.DIAMONDORGANICS.COM
WWW.FREIDAS.COM
WWW.MELISSAS.COM

### CAPERS

These tiny buds packed in brine add a pungent accent.

WWW.ADRIANASCARAVAN.COM
WWW.CHEFSHOP.COM
WWW.DITALIA.COM
WWW.ETHNICGROCER.COM
WWW.GLOBALFOODMARKET.COM

### CORNICHONS

Tiny sour pickles.

WWW.DEANDELUCA.COM
WWW.WINECHEESE.COM

### GREEN OLIVE TAPENADE

WWW.CYBERCUCINA.COM
WWW.DEANDELUCA.COM
WWW.DIAMONDORGANICS.COM

### HERBS, FRESH

(basil, cilantro, marjoram, mint, sage, etc.)

WWW.DIAMONDORGANICS.COM
WWW.THEFOODSTORES.COM

### MEYER LEMONS

A flavorful, sweet variety of lemon available in the spring.

WWW.DIAMONDORGANICS.COM

### MISO PASTE

A Japanese paste of fermented soybeans and rice or barley, used in soups, sauces, marinades, and dressings. May be listed online as soybean paste.

WWW.ADRIANASCARAVAN.COM
WWW.DIAMONDORGANICS.COM
WWW.GLOBALFOODMARKET.COM

### MUSHROOMS

Fresh and dried mushrooms, such as chanterelles, cremini, porcini, and cèpes. A large variety of "wild" mushrooms are now widely cultivated. Use in sauces, soups, salads, and on their own.

WWW.AUXDELICES.COM
WWW.DIAMONDORGANICS.COM
WWW.FRESHROOMS.COM
WWW.URBANI.COM

### PERSIMMONS, HACHIYA

Japanese variety that is sweet and slightly soft when ripe.

WWW.DIAMONDORGANICS.COM
WWW.MELISSAS.COM

### POMEGRANATES

WWW.DIAMONDORGANICS.COM
WWW.MELISSAS.COM

### POMEGRANATE JUICE

The tart-sweet juice of pomegranates is very difficult to extract—buy bottled juice.

WWW.KALUSTYANS.COM

### QUINCE PASTE, SPANISH MEMBRILLO

A thick jelly made from sweetened and cooked quince, traditionally served in Spain with manchego cheese.

WWW.ADRIANASCARAVAN.COM
WWW.CITARELLA.COM
WWW.CHEFSHOP.COM
WWW.MURRAYSCHEESE.COM
WWW.WORLDOFCHEESE.COM

### TAHINI

A thick paste made from crushed sesame seeds.

WWW.ADRIANASCARAVAN.COM
WWW.CHEFSHOP.COM
WWW.ETHNICGROCER.COM
WWW.GLOBALFOODMARKET.COM
WWW.SULTANSDELIGHT.COM

### TRUFFLES

Truffles, the most luxurious and expensive of wild—not cultivated—mushrooms. The best are black, from France, and white, from Italy.

WWW.CITARELLA.COM
WWW.DARTAGNAN.COM
WWW.URBANI.COM
WWW.WINECHEESE.COM

## MEAT, POULTRY, AND SEAFOOD

### BACON

The best bacon has a rich pork flavor and is not overly salty or fatty. My preference, from Niman Ranch, is made from pigs that are raised without hormones.

WWW.DARTAGNAN.COM
WWW.NIMANRANCH.COM
WWW.NUESKE.COM

### BEEF

WWW.CITARELLA.COM
WWW.LOBELS.COM
WWW.NIMANRANCH.COM

### CHICKEN, FREE-RANGE

Organic chickens raised without hormones or antibiotics.

WWW.DARTAGNAN.COM
WWW.MURRAYSCHICKENS.COM

### DEMI-GLACE

A rich reduction of stock cooked down to a glaze.

WWW.ADRIANASCARAVAN.COM
WWW.CHEFSHOP.COM
WWW.DEANDELUCA.COM
WWW.GLOBALFOODMARKET.COM

## DUCK, MUSCOVY

Muscovy is a much leaner breed than the more common Long Island duck. It doesn't require so much rendering or trimming of fat.
WWW.DARTAGNAN.COM
WWW.FRENCHSELECTIONS.COM
WWW.GRIMAUD.COM
WWW.HAUTEATHOME.COM

## FISH: HALIBUT, TUNA

Sushi-grade tuna is the best quality.
WWW.BROWNE-TRADING.COM
WWW.CITARELLA.COM

## FOIE GRAS

The enlarged liver of specially raised, fattened ducks and geese. Can be purchased in grades A, B, and C; use A or B only.
WWW.CITARELLA.COM
WWW.DARTAGNAN.COM
WWW.DEANDELUCA.COM
WWW.FRENCHSELECTIONS.COM
WWW.HAUTEATHOME.COM
WWW.HUDSONVALLEYFOIEGRAS.COM

## LAMB

Jamison Farm lamb is far superior in taste and is used by some of the best restaurants.
WWW.CITARELLA.COM
WWW.DARTAGNAN.COM
WWW.JAMISONFARM.COM
WWW.LOBELS.COM
WWW.NIMANRANCH.COM

## LOBSTER

The best and sweetest lobsters come from Maine.
WWW.BROWNE-TRADING.COM
WWW.CITARELLA.COM
WWW.FRESH-LOBSTERS.COM

## PANCETTA

Cured Italian bacon.
WWW.CITARELLA.COM

## PORK

My preference, from Niman Ranch, is made from pigs that are raised without hormones.
WWW.CITARELLA.COM
WWW.NIMANRANCH.COM

## PROSCIUTTO

Italian cured, dried ham. San Daniele is one of the best.
WWW.TEITELBROS.COM
WWW.URBANI.COM

## SCALLOPS, DIVER

Exceptionally sweet scallops that are harvested by hand.
WWW.BROWNE-TRADING.COM
WWW.CITARELLA.COM

## STOCKS

Some specialty-food markets sell stock.
WWW.CITARELLA.COM

## VEAL

WWW.CITARELLA.COM
WWW.LOBELS.COM

## VENISON

The farm-raised variety available for sale has a less gamey flavor than wild deer. Both are especially lean.
WWW.ATLANTICGAMEMEATS.COM
WWW.AVENISON.COM
WWW.CITARELLA.COM
WWW.HAUTEATHOME.COM

CHAPTER 2/
SIMPLY RAW TO BARELY COOKED

The dishes in this chapter are my favorite examples of "less is more," a phrase that could be the big city cook's mantra. Vibrant collages that seem to explode right off the plate, they retain their bright colors, true flavors, and interesting textures from crisp to creamy. Vegetables and seafood blend easily with accents such as fresh herbs and oils, and fruit combines equally well with sweet mint syrup, pomegranate molasses, honey, chiles, ginger, or pecorino cheese.

Fresh, uncooked foods are great ways to start a meal, almost like a taste of dessert before the entrée—I find them a much more appropriate beginning than anything rich. They also make uncomplicated main courses for lunches, picnics, or even small dinners. Raw and barely cooked foods allow the cook to focus on the quality of the ingredients and on the details that might get overlooked in more elaborate recipes. They are easier and quicker to make than cooked foods and often can be done in advance, freeing up the small apartment kitchen for other dinner-related tasks.

In raw and barely cooked recipes, high-quality ingredients are essential because you won't change them very much. When you shop for these foods, focus on their freshness, color, and texture—what you see is what you will get in the finished dish.

Unlike the other chapters, where you may sauté, roast, or simmer, here you will mostly slice, so be sure your best knives are sharpened and ready to go.

# ARUGULA
## WITH MANCHEGO, ROASTED ALMONDS, AND QUINCE DRESSING

SERVES 4 / In Spain, you might find quince paste (a firm jelly of quince and sugar) on a cheese plate, paired with savory manchego and some roasted almonds. This salad combines these typically Spanish flavors with crisp, slightly bitter arugula. You can eat a bowl of this as a full meal—I have, many times. | If you happen to have a citrus-flavored oil or nut oil in your pantry, use it instead of olive oil in the dressing, for added complexity.

### QUINCE DRESSING

1/4 CUP QUINCE PASTE (SEE SOURCES)

2 TABLESPOONS RED WINE VINEGAR

2 TABLESPOONS EXTRA-VIRGIN
    OLIVE OIL

1 TEASPOON FRESHLY SQUEEZED LEMON
    JUICE

KOSHER SALT

FRESHLY GROUND BLACK PEPPER

2 BUNCHES ARUGULA, TOUGH STEMS
    REMOVED

4 OUNCES MANCHEGO CHEESE, SHAVED

1/2 CUP ALMONDS, TOASTED (PAGE 18)
    AND COARSELY CHOPPED

### TO MAKE THE DRESSING

Put the quince paste and 1 tablespoon of the red wine vinegar in a medium nonreactive bowl. Use a whisk to break up the quince paste, and then whisk the mixture to a smooth consistency. Whisk in the remaining tablespoon of vinegar, the oil, and the lemon juice. Season with salt and pepper. The dressing can also be made in a blender, but it will emulsify, making it thicker and opaque. It will taste the same, but you may want to thin it with a little more red wine vinegar.

### TO ASSEMBLE THE SALAD

Just before serving, toss the arugula leaves with the dressing and most of the shaved manchego and chopped almonds. If you are using the thicker, emulsified dressing, toss the arugula gently, so the delicate leaves do not get weighed down. Divide the arugula among 4 serving plates and sprinkle with the remaining manchego and almonds.

# RAW MUSHROOM
## SALAD WITH FENNEL AND PARMESAN

SERVES 4 / This was inspired by a dish I tasted at Elio's, my favorite Italian restaurant, on Manhattan's Upper East Side. | The crunchiness of the fennel and the smoothness of the mushrooms make this salad a textural feast. It is sweet and savory at the same time and requires only a very simple dressing, with the Parmesan acting as a seasoning. Pile it gently on a plate and it will layer itself naturally; because each element is somewhat flat, the salad will resemble a mosaic.

1/2 POUND CREMINI MUSHROOMS, CAPS
    AND 1/4 INCH OF THE STEMS
1/2 CUP FRESHLY SQUEEZED LEMON
    JUICE
1 LARGE OR 2 SMALL BULBS FENNEL
1/4 CUP EXTRA-VIRGIN OLIVE OIL
1 TEASPOON WHITE TRUFFLE OIL
    (OPTIONAL; SEE SOURCES)
1/4 CUP COARSELY CHOPPED FLAT-LEAF
    PARSLEY
4 OUNCES SHAVED OR SHREDDED
    PARMESAN CHEESE (PREFERABLY
    PARMIGIANO-REGGIANO)
KOSHER SALT
FRESHLY GROUND BLACK PEPPER

Slice the mushrooms from top to bottom, approximately 1/8 inch thick. In a large nonreactive bowl, toss the mushrooms with half the lemon juice.

Halve the fennel lengthwise and remove and discard the tough inner core. Slice very thinly crosswise (use a mandoline, if you have one) and add to the mushrooms in the bowl. Add the remaining lemon juice, the olive oil, truffle oil, parsley, and Parmesan, and toss to combine. Season with salt and pepper.

# CARPACCIO OF CÈPES
## WITH WISCONSIN ASIAGO AND BALSAMIC SYRUP

SERVES 4 / Fall and winter are the seasons for cèpes (also called porcini), and although these mushrooms are expensive, they are worth every penny. Their flavor is woodsy and rich—like truffles, but with a little more body. (The flavor of truffles can sometime be elusive, but you can always taste cèpes.) They have a great chewy texture and an earthy aroma. Their creaminess is accented by Wisconsin Asiago cheese, with its hint of sharpness and its firm, moist texture.

**BALSAMIC SYRUP**
1 CUP BALSAMIC VINEGAR

**VINAIGRETTE**
JUICE AND GRATED ZEST OF 1 LEMON
2 TABLESPOONS WHITE TRUFFLE OIL
   (SEE SOURCES)
1/2 CUP EXTRA-VIRGIN OLIVE OIL
KOSHER SALT
FRESHLY GROUND BLACK PEPPER
1 BUNCH FLAT-LEAF PARSLEY, FINELY
   CHOPPED

**CARPACCIO**
1 POUND LARGE FRESH CÈPES (SEE
   SOURCES), CAPS ONLY, THINLY SLICED
   (1 POUND OF MUSHROOMS WILL YIELD
   ABOUT 1/2 POUND OF CAPS)
2 SCALLIONS, WHITE PARTS ONLY,
   THINLY SLICED
8 TO 12 THIN SLICES AGED ASIAGO
   CHEESE (4- TO 6-OUNCE PIECE)
1/4 CUP PINE NUTS, TOASTED (PAGE 18)

**TO MAKE THE BALSAMIC SYRUP**

In a small saucepan, heat the balsamic vinegar over medium heat until it begins to simmer. Reduce the heat to low and allow the vinegar to reduce gently until syrupy (about 30 minutes). Be sure to watch closely, as the reduced vinegar will burn easily. Cool to room temperature before using.

**TO MAKE THE VINAIGRETTE**

Place the lemon juice in a small bowl, slowly whisk in the oils, and season with salt and pepper. Add the chopped parsley and zest and mix well.

**TO ASSEMBLE THE CARPACCIO**

Arrange the mushrooms on 4 chilled plates. Brush generously with about half the vinaigrette, and season with salt and pepper. Sprinkle with the scallions. Top with the Asiago, drizzle with the remaining vinaigrette and the balsamic syrup, and sprinkle with the pine nuts.

# SASHIMI OF AVOCADO
## WITH LIME AND ALMOND OIL

*SERVES 4 /* Almond oil has a special affinity for the rich flavor and texture of avocado; its sweetness and aroma blend perfectly with that fruit. The best coarse salt, such as fleur de sel, sprinkled judiciously, will make the whole dish spring to life.

2 RIPE HASS AVOCADOS, HALVED
   LENGTHWISE, PITTED AND PEELED
JUICE OF 3 LIMES
$1/4$ CUP ALMOND OIL (SEE SOURCES),
   OR SUBSTITUTE WALNUT OR
   HAZELNUT OIL
FLEUR DE SEL, COARSE SEA SALT, OR
   KOSHER SALT
FRESHLY GROUND BLACK PEPPER
8 BASIL LEAVES, FINELY JULIENNED

Slice the avocado halves lengthwise about $1/8$ inch thick, and place on a baking sheet or large platter. Brush lightly on both sides with about half of the lime juice.

Divide the avocado slices among 4 chilled plates. Drizzle with the remaining lime juice and almond oil. Season with salt and pepper and top with the basil leaves.

TO PIT AND PEEL AN AVOCADO: CUT THE AVOCADO IN HALF LENGTH-WISE ALL THE WAY AROUND THE PIT, AND PULL INTO 2 HALVES. CAREFULLY STRIKE THE PIT WITH THE THICK END OF A CHEF'S KNIFE; GENTLY TWIST TO REMOVE THE PIT. WITH A SHARP KNIFE, GENTLY PEEL AWAY THE SKIN.

# ZUCCHINI CARPACCIO WITH BLACK TRUFFLE AND OLIVE OIL

SERVES 4 / I love this dish with a glass of chilled white wine on a hot summer's day. Pure simplicity, it satisfies without weighing you down and it lets you appreciate the delicate flavor of a single vegetable.

2 MEDIUM ZUCCHINI, ABOUT 1 POUND TOTAL, SLICED CROSSWISE 1/8 INCH THICK (USE A MANDOLINE OR SHARP KNIFE)

1/4 CUP EXTRA-VIRGIN OLIVE OIL

FLEUR DE SEL, COARSE SEA SALT, OR KOSHER SALT

FRESHLY GROUND BLACK PEPPER

1 BLACK TRUFFLE, SLICED PAPER THIN

2 OUNCES PARMESAN CHEESE (PREFERABLY PARMIGIANO-REGGIANO), SHAVED OR THINLY SLICED

2 TABLESPOONS AGED BALSAMIC VINEGAR

Arrange the zucchini slices to cover the surfaces of 4 plates. Brush with olive oil and season well with salt and pepper. Place the slices of truffle and Parmesan over the zucchini, and drizzle with the balsamic vinegar.

# TUNA SASHIMI
## WITH AVOCADO, LIME, AND CILANTRO

**SERVES 4** / This refreshing dish uses sparkling fresh ingredients and flavors and keeps each separate. Buy the best fish you can find—look for ruby red, firm, beautiful sushi-grade tuna, and be sure to keep the tuna and avocado well chilled.

2 RIPE HASS AVOCADOS, HALVED
    LENGTHWISE, PITTED AND PEELED
12 OUNCES SUSHI-GRADE TUNA, SLICED
    1/4 INCH THICK
1/4 CUP EXTRA-VIRGIN OLIVE OIL
1 LIME, HALVED CROSSWISE
FLEUR DE SEL, COARSE SEA SALT, OR
    KOSHER SALT
FRESHLY GROUND BLACK PEPPER
8 SPRIGS CILANTRO
2 SCALLIONS, THINLY SLICED (WHITE
    AND ABOUT 3 INCHES OF GREEN)

Slice the avocado halves crosswise about 1/4 inch thick. Divide the avocado slices among 4 chilled plates, cover with the tuna slices (see box), and drizzle with the olive oil. Just before serving, squeeze lime juice generously over all. (Don't do this earlier, because the lime juice immediately starts "cooking" the edges of the tuna.) Or squeeze the lime juice over the avocado slices before topping them with the tuna.

Sprinkle with salt and pepper. Garnish each plate with cilantro leaves and a scattering of sliced scallion.

> TO SLICE RAW TUNA: THE FISH MUST BE VERY COLD, AND THE KNIFE HAS TO BE SUPER SHARP. USE A LONG, THIN, NONSERRATED KNIFE, AND SLICE GENTLY WITHOUT APPLYING TOO MUCH PRESSURE. JUST LET THE KNIFE FALL THROUGH THE FISH.

# SUGAR-CURED SALMON WITH RICOTTA TOASTS

SERVES 12 TO 15 / Here is a lighter version of the classic lox and bagels, with ricotta standing in for the cream cheese, sugar-cured salmon replacing the saltier lox, and toasted brioche slices taking the place of bagels. This rendition makes a great appetizer or hors d'oeuvre, or even an open-faced sandwich. | Don't brush off all the cure before serving. It adds a crisp contrast to the velvety fish.

2 TABLESPOONS FENNEL SEED

1 SIDE OF SALMON (ABOUT 3 POUNDS),
    SKINNED AND FILLETED
    (THE FISHMONGER CAN DO THIS)

3 TABLESPOONS BRANDY

1/3 CUP KOSHER SALT

1/4 CUP SUGAR

1/4 CUP COARSELY CHOPPED MINT
    LEAVES

2 CUPS RICOTTA CHEESE

12 TO 15 SLICES BRIOCHE, TOASTED AND
    QUARTERED

MINT LEAVES, CHOPPED CHIVES,
    PARSLEY, OR CHERVIL (OPTIONAL)

In a small, dry pan over medium heat, gently toast the fennel seed until fragrant and browned, about 3 minutes, watching carefully to see that it does not burn. Remove from the heat and grind fine in a spice grinder or clean coffee grinder; or smash using a mortar and pestle.

Remove all the small pin bones from the salmon, using needle-nose pliers or tweezers. Lay the salmon on a large sheet of plastic wrap and rub with the brandy.

Combine the fennel seed, salt, and sugar, and rub all over the salmon. Spread the mint on top. Wrap the plastic tightly around the salmon, and then wrap with additional sheets of plastic. Place in a shallow nonreactive dish. Place another shallow pan on top of the salmon and weigh it down with a brick or several heavy cans. Refrigerate for 24 to 48 hours; unwrap every 12 to 14 hours and baste with the accumulated juices. The salmon is done when it feels firm and the surface is shiny and opaque.

Slice the salmon crosswise (see box). Spread the ricotta on the toasted brioche slices and top with slices of salmon. Garnish with the herbs, if desired.

---

TO SLICE THE SALMON: USE A LONG, THIN, NONSERRATED KNIFE. BEGIN AT ONE END OF THE FISH, CUTTING AT A 45-DEGREE ANGLE. TO GET TRANSPARENT SLICES, PUT YOUR HAND ON TOP OF THE SALMON, PRESS DOWN GENTLY, AND RUN THE KNIFE JUST UNDER YOUR HAND.

# BLACK BASS
# SEVICHE WITH MANGO AND GINGER

SERVES 4 / Your first taste of this dish will whisk you to the tropics or a sunny beach. The spiciness of the ginger and chile combines with the sweetness of the mango and coconut milk, providing a lovely balance of flavors. This is light, cleansing, and refreshing.

3/4 POUND BLACK BASS FILLET, SKIN REMOVED (YOUR FISHMONGER CAN DO THIS) AND CUT INTO 1/2-INCH DICE, OR SUBSTITUTE RED SNAPPER

1 CUP FRESHLY SQUEEZED LIME JUICE

2 TEASPOONS SUGAR

1/2 TEASPOON FLEUR DE SEL OR COARSE SEA SALT

1 (14-OUNCE) CAN UNSWEETENED COCONUT MILK, STRAINED (SEE NOTE)

1/2 CUP FINELY DICED JICAMA (1/2 MEDIUM JICAMA)

2 TABLESPOONS FINELY DICED RED ONION (1/2 SMALL ONION)

1 TABLESPOON MINCED SERRANO CHILE (1 CHILE)

1 TABLESPOON MINCED PEELED FRESH GINGER

1 RIPE MANGO, PEELED AND CUT INTO 1/2-INCH DICE

1/4 CUP MINT LEAVES, CUT INTO THIN RIBBONS

In a medium nonreactive bowl, combine the bass with the lime juice. Cover and marinate in the refrigerator for 2 to 3 hours.

Drain the marinade from the bass. In a small bowl, combine the sugar, salt, and coconut milk. Pour over the bass. Add the jicama, onion, chile, ginger, half of the mango, and half of the mint, and combine well.

Divide the seviche among 4 chilled shallow bowls or martini glasses and garnish with the remaining mango and mint.

NOTE

Start with 1 can unsweetened coconut milk and remove the fat. If the fat has solidified, scoop it out with a spoon, or strain the milk through cheesecloth or a fine strainer. The milk should be as thin and clear as possible; when it is strained, you should have about 1/2 can of liquid.

# SEVICHE OF DIVER SCALLOPS
## WITH CHIVE DRESSING

SERVES 4 / Diver scallops, also known as dayboat scallops on the West Coast, are harvested by hand, as opposed to being gathered by net. The best are sold as dry diver scallops, and they are worth searching for. Because they are not preserved in brine, they are sweet with an oceany, oysterlike flavor. I wouldn't use anything else for this recipe, which is clean, pure, and refreshing.

### SEVICHE

$1^1/2$ CUPS FRESH LIME JUICE

GRATED ZEST OF 2 LIMES

2 TEASPOONS GRATED FRESH HORSERADISH

2 TEASPOONS SUGAR

1 TEASPOON TABASCO SAUCE OR CHILI OIL

2 TEASPOONS KOSHER SALT, PLUS ADDITIONAL FOR SPRINKLING

8 LARGE DIVER SCALLOPS (ABOUT 12 OUNCES), SLICED CROSSWISE INTO $1/4$-INCH DISKS, TOUGH MUSCLE REMOVED FROM THE SIDE OF EACH SCALLOP, IF NECESSARY

### CHIVE DRESSING

$3/4$ CUP EXTRA-VIRGIN OLIVE OIL, PLUS ADDITIONAL FOR BRUSHING BREAD

1 BUNCH CHIVES, COARSELY CHOPPED (ABOUT 1 CUP), PLUS $1/4$ CUP FINELY CHOPPED CHIVES

### TOAST

8 THIN SLICES SOURDOUGH BREAD

1 SMALL DAIKON OR ICICLE RADISH (4 TO 6 OUNCES) SLICED CROSSWISE $1/16$ INCH THICK

4 CUPS LOOSELY PACKED BABY GREENS

### TO MAKE THE SEVICHE

In a medium nonreactive bowl, combine the lime juice (reserve 1 teaspoon of the juice for the dressing), zest, horseradish, sugar, Tabasco sauce, and 1 teaspoon of the salt. Lay the scallops in one layer in a wide, shallow, nonreactive bowl, and cover with the lime juice mixture. It's very important that all the scallops are covered by lime juice. While they are marinating, move them around a few times to make sure they don't stick together. (If that happens they won't marinate evenly, and some may end up raw.) Cover with plastic wrap and refrigerate for 1 to $1^1/2$ hours. The scallops are done when they have turned opaque.

### TO MAKE THE CHIVE DRESSING

Combine the $3/4$ cup of oil, 1 cup of the coarsley chopped chives, the reserved 1 teaspoon lime juice, and the remaining 1 teaspoon salt in a blender and purée until smooth. Taste and add more salt if necessary. Set aside.

### TO MAKE THE TOASTS

Preheat the broiler or toaster oven. Brush the slices of sourdough with olive oil, season with salt, and toast under the broiler until golden on both sides.

### TO SERVE

Divide the scallops among 4 chilled plates, arranging them in a circle. Top with the radishes. Spoon a few tablespoons of the marinade over the scallops and radishes, and place a handful of baby greens in the center. Drizzle with the chive dressing and sprinkle with the finely chopped chives. Serve with the sourdough toasts.

### VARIATION

Substitute an equal amount of cilantro for chives in the dressing, and garnish with chopped cilantro.

# SHRIMP SEVICHE WITH FENNEL AND POMEGRANATE

*SERVES 4 /* In this variation on a traditional seviche, shrimp are blanched and then briefly marinated in olive oil and citrus juices, leaving them juicy and firm. Crisp fennel and scallions, fresh mint, and pomegranate add flavor and crunch.

1 POUND LARGE SHRIMP (16 TO 20), PEELED AND DEVEINED

1/2 CUP FRESHLY SQUEEZED LIME JUICE

1/2 CUP FRESHLY SQUEEZED ORANGE JUICE

1/4 CUP EXTRA-VIRGIN OLIVE OIL

2 TEASPOONS KOSHER SALT

FRESHLY GROUND BLACK PEPPER

1 SMALL FENNEL BULB, JULIENNED LENGTHWISE

2 SCALLIONS, THINLY SLICED (WHITE AND ABOUT 3 INCHES OF GREEN)

2 TABLESPOONS JULIENNED MINT LEAVES

2 TABLESPOONS POMEGRANATE MOLASSES (SEE SOURCES)

2 TABLESPOONS POMEGRANATE SEEDS (OPTIONAL)

Fill a large bowl with ice water and set aside. Bring a large pot of salted water to a boil, add the shrimp, and remove from the heat. Let stand for 1 minute; then drain the shrimp and immediately plunge them into ice water to stop the cooking. Cut the shrimp into small dice and set aside.

In a medium nonreactive bowl, whisk together the citrus juices, olive oil, salt, and pepper. Add the shrimp, fennel, and scallions, and refrigerate for 30 minutes to 1 hour. Drain off most of the marinade, and toss the seviche with the mint.

Divide the shrimp mixture among 4 serving plates and drizzle with half of the pomegranate molasses. Drizzle the remaining molasses decoratively around the plate, sprinkle with pomegranate seeds, if desired, and serve immediately.

# LOBSTER SEVICHE WITH RED CHILE DRESSING

SERVES 4 / The texture and sweetness of this seviche are amazing, because you lightly under-cook the lobster and then let the citric acid in the dressing finish the "cooking." If you were to use fully cooked lobsters, the dressing would toughen the tender meat, but this balance of methods brings it to exactly the right point. | Lemon cucumbers are thin skinned and juicy but sometimes hard to find. Kirby or hothouse cucumbers make good substitutes.

## LOBSTERS

2 LIVE LOBSTERS, 1¹/₂ TO 2 POUNDS
    EACH

## DRESSING

¹/₃ CUP FRESHLY SQUEEZED LIME JUICE

1 FRESH RED CHILE, SUCH AS SERRANO
    OR POBLANO, SPLIT, SEEDED, AND
    MINCED

¹/₄ CUP FINELY CHOPPED CILANTRO

¹/₄ CUP EXTRA-VIRGIN OLIVE OIL

KOSHER SALT

FRESHLY GROUND BLACK PEPPER

1 RIPE HASS AVOCADO, PEELED, PITTED,
    AND CUT INTO LARGE DICE

1 SMALL LEMON CUCUMBER, PEELED
    AND SLICED CROSSWISE ¹/₈-INCH
    THICK, OR SUBSTITUTE 1 KIRBY OR
    ¹/₂ HOTHOUSE CUCUMBER

2 SCALLIONS, THINLY SLICED (WHITE
    AND ABOUT 3 INCHES OF GREEN)

### TO COOK THE LOBSTERS

Fill a large bowl with ice water and set aside. Bring a large pot of salted water to a boil and add the lobsters, head first. Boil for 5 to 6 minutes; remove the lobsters from the pot and plunge them into the ice water to stop the cooking. The lobsters should be slightly undercooked. Remove the tail and claw meat and chop into ¹/₂-inch dice.

### TO MAKE THE DRESSING

In a small nonreactive bowl, whisk the lime juice with the chile and cilantro; then slowly whisk in the olive oil. Season with salt and pepper.

### TO ASSEMBLE THE SALAD

In a large nonreactive bowl, gently combine the lobster meat, avocado, and red chile dressing. Taste and reseason, if necessary. Refrigerate for 8 to 10 minutes before serving.

    Arrange a thin layer of cucumber on each of 4 serving plates and pile the lobster seviche on top, reserving any dressing that remains in the bowl. Sprinkle with the scallions and drizzle the reserved dressing around the lobster.

# PROSCIUTTO AND BLUE CHEESE PANINI
## WITH WHITE TRUFFLE HONEY

**SERVES 4 /** In this simple but heavenly combination, top-quality ingredients stand out. LuLu White Truffle Honey (from Restaurant LuLu of San Francisco) is an incredible product. Substitute another superior honey if you must—the sandwich won't be the same, but it will still be good. San Daniele, an outstanding Italian prosciutto, is relatively easy to find, as is Parma prosciutto. For the blue cheese, look for something slightly on the drier side; Great Hill Blue is excellent in this recipe.

1 BAGUETTE, CUT LENGTHWISE
  3/4 THROUGH AND THEN QUARTERED
  CROSSWISE
1/4 CUP EXTRA-VIRGIN OLIVE OIL
10 OUNCES THINLY SLICED ITALIAN
  PROSCIUTTO, SUCH AS SAN DANIELE
  OR PARMA (SEE SOURCES)
1 RIPE BOSC PEAR, CORED AND THINLY
  SLICED (DO NOT PEEL)
1/4 CUP LULU WHITE TRUFFLE HONEY
  (SEE SOURCES), OR SUBSTITUTE
  ANOTHER HONEY
FRESHLY GROUND BLACK PEPPER
12 BASIL LEAVES, TORN INTO PIECES
4 OUNCES GOOD-QUALITY BLUE CHEESE,
  SUCH AS GREAT HILL (SEE SOURCES),
  CRUMBLED

Lightly toast the baguette, brush the inside of the baguette with olive oil, and line with the prosciutto slices. Cover with the pear slices. Brush the pear with the honey, season with pepper, and top with the basil leaves. Sprinkle with the blue cheese, close the sandwiches, and serve.

# CHARRED BEEF CARPACCIO
## WITH ASPARAGUS AND MANCHEGO

SERVES 4 / Carpaccio is usually paired with arugula and Parmesan, but in this milder take, I substitute sweet asparagus for the slightly bitter arugula and creamy manchego for the Parmesan. Be sure to use a younger manchego, aged not more than 2 months. | There is great texture, as well as extra flavor, in this combination. And to add a bit more of both, the carpaccio is quickly seared over high heat. It forms a well-browned crust, but the meat remains raw inside. If you have trouble slicing the meat thin, rewrap it and place it in the freezer for half an hour, until it becomes firm. Before serving, make sure the beef slices have returned to room temperature.

3 TABLESPOONS COARSELY CRACKED BLACK PEPPERCORNS (WRAP THEM IN A DISH TOWEL AND SMASH WITH A HEAVY PAN)

12 OUNCES BEEF TENDERLOIN, TRIMMED OF FAT

KOSHER SALT

4 TABLESPOONS EXTRA-VIRGIN OLIVE OIL

16 SPEARS THIN ASPARAGUS, TRIMMED AND PEELED

4 TABLESPOONS AGED BALSAMIC VINEGAR

4 OUNCES YOUNG MANCHEGO CHEESE, SHAVED (USE A VEGETABLE PEELER) OR VERY THINLY SLICED

1/4 CUP MINCED CHIVES

FRESHLY GROUND BLACK PEPPER

Place a medium cast-iron skillet over high heat until very hot (4 to 5 minutes). Spread the cracked peppercorns on a large plate. Season the beef with salt and then roll it in the peppercorns, coating it evenly. Add 2 tablespoons of the olive oil to the skillet and sear the beef on all sides until well charred, about 2 minutes per side. Refrigerate for at least 1 hour or up to 6 hours.

Fill a large bowl with ice water and set aside. Bring a large pot of salted water to a boil. Add the asparagus to the boiling water and cook until just tender and still bright green, 2 to 3 minutes. Drain the asparagus and plunge it into the ice water to cool; drain well. Slice the spears diagonally into 2-inch lengths. Put the asparagus in a medium nonreactive bowl and add the remaining 2 tablespoons olive oil, 2 tablespoons of the balsamic vinegar, the cheese, and half the chives. Season with salt and pepper and toss to combine.

With a very sharp knife, slice the beef crosswise as thin as possible, no more than 1/8 inch thick. Arrange the slices on 4 plates and top with the asparagus and cheese mixture. Drizzle with the remaining 2 tablespoons balsamic vinegar, and sprinkle with the remaining chives.

# RIPE PERSIMMONS WITH MINT SYRUP

SERVES 4 / When you shop for persimmons, you will find two distinct types. The Fuyu, with a squat, compact shape much like a tomato, is firm. The Hachiya or Japanese persimmon has a dome-shaped top and a creamy texture and is soft, sweet, and slightly tart when ripe, but astringent if unripe. Use the softer, sweeter Hachiya for this recipe.

$2/3$ CUP WATER

$1/2$ CUP SUGAR

$1/4$ CUP MINT LEAVES

2 RIPE HACHIYA OR JAPANESE
  PERSIMMONS, PEELED AND SLICED
  $1/4$ INCH THICK, OR SUBSTITUTE
  RIPE PAPAYA OR MANGO

In a small saucepan, combine the water and sugar and bring to a boil over high heat. Add the mint, reserving 8 leaves for garnish, and simmer for 2 minutes. Remove from the heat and let steep for 10 minutes. Strain the syrup and discard the mint leaves.

Divide the persimmons among 4 plates. Drizzle with the mint syrup and garnish with the reserved mint leaves.

# STRAWBERRIES
## WITH POMEGRANATE MOLASSES AND FRESH RICOTTA

**SERVES 4** / This seemingly simple recipe is about selecting perfect ingredients as much as it is about preparing them. Take the time to find ripe, beautiful red strawberries; go to a Middle Eastern market or look on the Web for some pomegranate molasses; and get a really good fresh ricotta instead of a commercially processed type. The result of your efforts will be a dish that tastes phenomenal.

1 QUART RIPE STRAWBERRIES, STEMMED
    AND HALVED
2 TABLESPOONS SUGAR
GRATED ZEST OF 1 LEMON
1 TABLESPOON FRESHLY SQUEEZED
    LEMON JUICE
KOSHER SALT
1 CUP WHOLE MILK RICOTTA CHEESE
2 TABLESPOONS POMEGRANATE
    MOLASSES (SEE SOURCES), OR
    SUBSTITUTE BALSAMIC SYRUP
    (PAGE 39)
12 MINT LEAVES

In a large bowl, toss the strawberries with the sugar. Whisk the lemon zest, lemon juice, and a pinch of salt into the ricotta. Divide the strawberries among 4 bowls, top with the ricotta mixture, drizzle with the pomegranate molasses, and garnish with the mint leaves.

# PEARS
## WITH HONEY, WALNUT TOAST, AND PECORINO

*SERVES 4 /* In this perfect finale to a rustic meal, brown-skinned Bosc pears, sugary and crisp, offer the best contrast to a creamy pecorino (the young, mild cheese, not the aged, harder type). If you choose a more buttery pear, such as Comice, the flavor will be there but you won't have a textural foil for the cheese. A dense walnut bread adds crunch and chew to the composition. | This dish also makes a simple light lunch or afternoon snack.

8 SLICES PECORINO TOSCANO CHEESE, ABOUT 1/8 INCH THICK

2 RIPE BOSC PEARS, UNPEELED, CORED AND CUT INTO 8 WEDGES EACH, OR SUBSTITUTE COMICE OR FORELLE PEARS

8 THIN SLICES DENSE WALNUT BREAD, TOASTED, OR SUBSTITUTE SOURDOUGH

1/4 CUP HONEY

1/2 CUP WALNUTS, TOASTED (PAGE 18) AND COARSELY CHOPPED

COARSELY CRACKED BLACK PEPPER

Place a slice of cheese and 2 pear wedges on each toast. Drizzle with honey, sprinkle with the chopped walnuts and cracked pepper, and serve. Or arrange the toasts, cheese, and pears on a large serving platter. Accompany with small bowls of the honey, walnuts, and cracked pepper and serve, allowing your guests to assemble their own toasts.

# SPICED FRUIT SOUP
## WITH GINGER AND TOASTED ALMOND ICE CREAM

SERVES 4 / This fragrant, colorful dessert is perfect to serve to guests, since the components can be made in advance and assembled at the last minute. The spiced syrup adds an exotic accent to fresh, ripe fruits and berries. This syrup also makes the base for a refreshing drink; see Spiced Summer Limeade, page 58. | Use the fruits listed here or substitute your favorites—or the most beautiful specimens your market has to offer.

### SYRUP

2 CUPS SUGAR

2 1/2 CUPS WATER

2 TABLESPOONS CARDAMOM PODS, SHELLS CRACKED

6 STAR ANISE, IN SMALL PIECES

3 SLICES PEELED FRESH GINGER, EACH ABOUT THE SIZE OF A NICKEL

1/2 VANILLA BEAN, SPLIT LENGTHWISE

### ICE CREAM

1 PINT VANILLA ICE CREAM

3 TABLESPOONS FINELY CHOPPED CANDIED GINGER (SEE SOURCES)

1/4 CUP COARSELY CHOPPED TOASTED ALMONDS (PAGE 18)

### FRUIT SOUP

2 LARGE NECTARINES OR PEACHES, PITTED AND THINLY SLICED

2 TO 3 PLUMS, PITTED AND THINLY SLICED

1/4 POUND SWEET, DARK CHERRIES, PITTED

1/2 PINT STRAWBERRIES, STEMS REMOVED, HALVED, OR QUARTERED IF LARGE

2 KIWI FRUIT, PEELED, SLICED CROSS-WISE, AND THE SLICES QUARTERED

1/4 FRESH PINEAPPLE, THINLY SLICED

1/2 PINT BLUEBERRIES

2 TABLESPOONS COARSELY CHOPPED MINT, PLUS 4 MINT SPRIGS FOR GARNISH

### TO MAKE THE SYRUP

In a medium saucepan over medium-high heat, combine the sugar, water, cardamom pods, star anise, ginger, and vanilla bean. Bring to a boil and cook, stirring occasionally, until the sugar dissolves. Decrease the heat to as low as possible, and cook for about 1 hour. Strain the syrup into a medium bowl and discard the solids (or, to intensify the flavors, refrigerate the syrup overnight before straining out the solids). You should have about 4 cups.

### TO MAKE THE ICE CREAM

While the syrup is cooking, remove the ice cream from the freezer to soften slightly. Put the ice cream, candied ginger, and toasted almonds in a medium bowl and stir to combine thoroughly. Spoon the ice cream back into its container and return to the freezer. Freeze until solid.

### TO MAKE THE FRUIT SOUP

One to 2 hours before serving, put the nectarines, plums, and cherries into the syrup. This will soften the fruits and give the syrup a reddish color.

Just before serving, divide the syrup and fruit mixture among 4 shallow soup bowls. Divide the strawberries, kiwi fruit, pineapple, and blueberries among the 4 bowls. Sprinkle with the chopped mint. Place a scoop of the ice cream in the center of each bowl, garnish with a mint sprig, and serve.

# SPICED SUMMER LIMEADE

SERVES 4 / The syrup from the Spiced Fruit Soup (page 57) provides the basis for this wonderfully tart limeade.

## SYRUP

1 CUP SUGAR

1¼ CUPS WATER

1 TABLESPOON CARDAMOM PODS, SHELLS CRACKED

3 WHOLE STAR ANISE, BROKEN INTO PIECES

2 SLICES PEELED FRESH GINGER, EACH ABOUT THE SIZE OF A NICKEL

¼ VANILLA BEAN, SPLIT LENGTHWISE

## LIMEADE

1 CUP FRESHLY SQUEEZED LIME JUICE

2 CUPS WATER OR SPARKLING WATER

4 SPRIGS MINT

### TO MAKE THE SYRUP

In a medium saucepan over medium-high heat, combine the sugar, water, cardamom pods, star anise, ginger, and vanilla bean. Bring to a boil and cook, stirring occasionally, until the sugar dissolves. Decrease the heat to as low as possible, and cook for about 1 hour. Allow to cool before making the limeade. You should have about 2 cups syrup.

Strain the syrup into a medium bowl and discard the solids (or, to intensify the flavors, refrigerate the syrup overnight before straining out the solids).

### TO MAKE THE LIMEADE

In a large pitcher, combine the syrup, lime juice, and water. Serve in tall glasses over lots of ice. Garnish each serving with a mint sprig.

# CHAPTER 3/ FLASHES IN THE PAN

# FLASHES IN THE PAN

Of all the methods of cooking, sautéing provides the closest thing to instant gratification: The ingredients are right there in front of you, and you can watch their transformation as the dish progresses. Before your very eyes, a hazelnut-crusted slice of foie gras or some scallops, tuna, or beef filet sears to a golden color and starts to release savory aromas. The food retains much of its natural shape and texture, and the resulting dish is beautiful as well as flavorful and juicy. And what could be more natural? A cook's first instinct is simply to heat up a pan and put something in it.

The style is quick and easy, but there is plenty of room for spin. Portobello mushrooms stand in for chicken or veal when they are coated with almonds and bread crumbs and sautéed, and the result is light yet hearty. Golden caramelized cauliflower and brown butter vinaigrette add perfect satiny notes to simple seared scallops. Crisp asparagus and juicy blood oranges provide ideal accessories for sweet lobster, and sautéed chicken breasts are enriched with chile, lime, and honey in a sweet and sour glaze. Ripe, juicy cherries are deeply flavored with a sweet reduction of red wine and a touch of vanilla and combined with crème fraîche for an eye-catching dessert.

This chapter will teach city cooks a valuable lesson: how to add deep, rich flavor, without a lot of work and time. In addition to learning about the sautéing process itself, you'll learn how to transform every dish with herbs, spices, citrus, and sweet and savory additions.

As for technique, I can offer a few useful tips: Don't start cooking in a cold pan! Allow your sauté pan and the cooking oil in it enough time to get hot—the food should sizzle when it hits the pan. Be careful not to cook in a wet pan or to let water fall into a sauté, to avoid splatters. If you are including honey or any kind of sweet baste, add it at the end so it does not burn. And forget the common misconception that you always have to shake the pan and move it around over the fire. If you are cooking fish or meat, let it sit and brown for a while, and it will be uniformly cooked—sautéing doesn't have to be a workout.

# PORTOBELLO PICCATA
## WITH ALMOND BREAD CRUMBS, ROSEMARY, AND BALSAMIC VINAIGRETTE

SERVES 4 AS A FIRST COURSE / A piccata would normally be made with chicken or veal, but portobello mushrooms have enough texture and flavor to be a good meat substitute. To contrast with that texture, we add an almond crust, and fresh rosemary and a balsamic vinaigrette enhance the earthy flavor.

4 LARGE PORTOBELLO MUSHROOMS

1 CUP FRESH COARSE BREAD CRUMBS, PREFERABLY FROM BRIOCHE

1¼ CUPS BLANCHED ALMONDS, TOASTED (PAGE 18) AND COARSELY CHOPPED

2 TABLESPOONS FINELY CHOPPED ROSEMARY

1 TABLESPOON GRATED LEMON ZEST

KOSHER SALT

FRESHLY GROUND BLACK PEPPER

²/₃ CUP FLOUR

3 EGGS

3 TABLESPOONS PLUS ½ TEASPOON FRESHLY SQUEEZED LEMON JUICE

5 TABLESPOONS EXTRA-VIRGIN OLIVE OIL

1 TABLESPOON PLUS 1 TEASPOON AGED BALSAMIC VINEGAR

6 CUPS LOOSELY PACKED BABY SPINACH OR ARUGULA

2 TABLESPOONS COARSELY CHOPPED FLAT-LEAF PARSLEY

Wipe the mushrooms clean with a wet cloth. Cut off the stems as close to the base as possible. Carefully slice off the slightly rounded top part of each cap, so that the mushrooms are as flat and even as possible and about ¾ to 1 inch thick. This is necessary to create a flat surface that will brown evenly.

In a large, shallow bowl, combine the bread crumbs, 1 cup of the chopped almonds, the rosemary, and the lemon zest, and season with salt and pepper. Place the flour in a separate shallow bowl. Whisk the eggs in a third shallow bowl with 3 tablespoons of the lemon juice.

Dip each mushroom in the flour and shake off any excess. Then dip it in the egg, allowing the excess to drip off. Finally, dip it into the bread crumb mixture to coat, and set aside.

In a large skillet (preferably nonstick) over medium-high heat, heat 3 tablespoons of the olive oil. Decrease the heat to medium and brown the mushrooms on both sides, pressing down on them gently with a spatula to help the crumb mixture to stick. Cook for about 5 minutes per side, until they are cooked through, decreasing the heat further if necessary to make sure the crust does not burn. Remove the mushrooms from the skillet and drain on paper towels.

In a medium nonreactive bowl, whisk together the balsamic vinegar, the remaining ½ teaspoon lemon juice, and the remaining 2 tablespoons olive oil. Season with salt and pepper. In a large bowl, dress the greens with half of the vinaigrette, or just enough so they are lightly coated. Divide among 4 plates. Place the mushrooms on top. Drizzle with some of the remaining vinaigrette and sprinkle with chopped parsley and the remaining ¼ cup chopped almonds.

# HAZELNUT-CRUSTED FOIE GRAS WITH FENNEL AND POMEGRANATE

SERVES 4 / I love the flavor of foie gras, but I think the texture could be a bit more exciting, and that's the reason for the hazelnuts. Their crunchiness brings an elegant, luxurious dish down to earth, and the sweet-tart note of pomegranate molasses ties everything together. This makes a pretty plate, with its earth tones, reds, and whites. I've done dozens of variations on hazelnut-crusted foie gras in the last ten years, but this one is my favorite.

12 OUNCES FOIE GRAS (SEE SOURCES)

2 BLOOD ORANGES (OR SUBSTITUTE
   1 RED GRAPEFRUIT)

KOSHER SALT

FRESHLY GROUND BLACK PEPPER

1 CUP HAZELNUTS, TOASTED (PAGE 18),
   SKINNED, AND COARSELY CHOPPED
   (SEE NOTE)

4 CUPS LOOSELY PACKED BABY GREENS

1/2 BULB FENNEL, CORE REMOVED,
   FINELY JULIENNED

1 TABLESPOON EXTRA-VIRGIN OLIVE OIL

1/4 CUP POMEGRANATE MOLASSES (SEE
   SOURCES), AGED BALSAMIC VINEGAR,
   OR BALSAMIC SYRUP (PAGE 39)

If using whole foie gras, carefully separate the two lobes. Using a small, sharp knife, cut away any membrane, large veins, and excess fat.

Using a sharp, thin knife held briefly under hot running water and then wiped dry, gently cut the foie gras into slices approximately 1/2 inch thick. Wrap with plastic and refrigerate. Keep the foie gras wrapped and well chilled until ready to cook.

Cut off both ends of each orange and cut away the peel, using a small paring knife. Working over a bowl to catch any juices, gently cut along each side of the membranes to separate the segments. Place the segments in the bowl and squeeze in any juice remaining from the oranges.

Gently score the the foie gras slices on both sides (about 1/16 inch deep), and season with salt and pepper. Heat a large skillet over high heat until very hot; decrease the heat to medium-high and place the foie gras slices in the dry pan. Cook until golden brown, about 1 minute, then gently flip the slices over. While the other side is cooking, press the chopped hazelnuts into the cooked side of the slices. After the second side has cooked for about 1 minute, remove from the heat. Be careful not to cook it for too long or at too high a temperature, to avoid melting it.

To serve, combine the greens, fennel, and orange sections, with juice, in a large bowl. Drizzle with the olive oil, season with salt and pepper, and toss gently. Divide among 4 serving plates, top with the foie gras slices, and drizzle with the pomegranate molasses.

NOTE

To skin whole toasted hazelnuts, wrap them in a clean dish towel and rub them. Most of the skin will come off.

# PAN-COOKED MUSSELS

**SERVES 4 AS A FIRST COURSE, 2 AS A MAIN COURSE /** Having grown up in Maine eating freshly gathered shellfish, I find this dish brings back special memories. One of my favorite things to serve at a city party, these mussels can simply be piled high in a big bowl in the center of the table. Give your guests plenty of fresh, crusty bread to dip into the delicious broth, and make sure you have a generous supply of chilled white wine. Of course, provide lots of napkins, along with plates for the discarded shells.

2 TABLESPOONS EXTRA-VIRGIN OLIVE
OIL, PLUS ADDITIONAL FOR BRUSHING
THE BREAD

2 SHALLOTS, FINELY CHOPPED (ABOUT
$1/2$ CUP)

$3/4$ CUP WHITE WINE

$1^1/2$ CUPS VEGETABLE STOCK OR
CANNED LOW-SODIUM BROTH

2 POUNDS MUSSELS, CLEANED AND
BEARDED

4 SLICES RUSTIC BREAD

KOSHER SALT

$1/4$ CUP FINELY CHOPPED FLAT-LEAF
PARSLEY

FRESHLY GROUND BLACK PEPPER

Preheat the broiler.

Heat the 2 tablespoons of olive oil in a large, heavy pot over medium-high heat. Add the shallots and cook, stirring occasionally, until translucent, about 3 minutes. Add the wine and cook until reduced by half, about 3 minutes. Add the stock and mussels, cover, and steam until the mussels open, about 7 minutes.

Meanwhile, brush the bread slices with olive oil and sprinkle lightly with salt. Toast the bread under the broiler or in a toaster oven and set aside.

Remove the mussels from the heat and discard any that have not opened. Using a slotted spoon, transfer the mussels to shallow soup bowls or other rimmed serving dishes, and sprinkle generously with parsley. Season the cooking liquid with salt and pepper and pour over the mussels. Serve with the toasted bread.

# SAUTÉED LOBSTER
## WITH ASPARAGUS AND BLOOD ORANGES

SERVES 4 / The delicacy of quickly blanched lobster pairs beautifully with crisp, fresh asparagus, aromatic basil, and intense blood oranges. Although this is a simple dish, the flambé adds a luxurious touch.

2 BLOOD ORANGES

4 LIVE LOBSTERS, ABOUT 1 1/2 POUNDS
    EACH

12 TO 16 THIN SPEARS ASPARAGUS,
    TOUGH ENDS CUT AWAY, CUT
    DIAGONALLY INTO 2-INCH LENGTHS

5 TABLESPOONS BUTTER

KOSHER SALT

FRESHLY GROUND BLACK PEPPER

1/2 CUP GRAND MARNIER LIQUEUR

1/4 CUP LOOSELY PACKED BASIL LEAVES,
    CUT INTO THIN RIBBONS

### TO SEGMENT THE BLOOD ORANGES

Cut the peel from the top and bottom and stand each orange upright on a cutting board. With a small, sharp paring knife, gently slice away the peel down to the flesh. Cut along each side of the membranes to separate the segments, and reserve the segments in a small bowl.

### TO COOK THE LOBSTERS AND ASPARAGUS

Fill a large bowl with ice water. Bring a large pot of salted water to a boil.

Cook the lobsters in the pot (you may need to do 2 at a time if the pot is not large enough for all 4), covered, for 4 minutes. Drain the lobsters and plunge them into the ice water to cool. Drain again, remove the tail and claw meat, and slice each tail into 3 or 4 pieces.

Refill the bowl with ice water. Bring a medium pot of salted water to a boil and cook the asparagus for 2 minutes. Drain the asparagus and plunge it into the ice water to stop the cooking. Drain again and set aside.

Melt 4 tablespoons of the butter in a large skillet over medium-high heat. Add the lobster, season with salt and pepper, and sauté for about 2 minutes.

Remove the lobster from the heat and pour the Grand Marnier over it. Ignite it with a lighted match, gently ease the skillet back onto the flame, and cook for 2 minutes. Add the asparagus, toss to heat through, and stir in the remaining tablespoon of butter.

### TO SERVE

Place a few pieces of asparagus on each of 4 plates and top with the lobster and the remaining asparagus. Arrange the blood orange sections on and around the lobster. Drizzle with the Grand Marnier butter remaining in the pan, and garnish with the basil.

# SEARED SCALLOPS
## WITH CARAMELIZED CAULIFLOWER AND BROWN BUTTER VINAIGRETTE

SERVES 4 / In this attractive dish, the scallops are seared until golden. The cauliflower is blanched in a saffron-infused broth to make it a beautiful yellow, and then it is caramelized (after you've cooked the cauliflower, you can save the saffron-infused stock and use it in preparing saffron rice). The sauce is a flavorful vinaigrette made with brown butter, lemon, and chicken stock.

### CAULIFLOWER

7 CUPS CHICKEN STOCK OR CANNED
   LOW-SODIUM BROTH, OR 5 CUPS
   WATER PLUS 2 CUPS CHICKEN STOCK
   OR BROTH
2 TEASPOONS SAFFRON THREADS
1/2 LARGE OR 1 SMALL HEAD
   CAULIFLOWER, FLORETS HALVED
   LENGTHWISE

5 TABLESPOONS BUTTER

### VINAIGRETTE

1 TEASPOON DIJON MUSTARD
1 TABLESPOON FRESHLY SQUEEZED
   LEMON JUICE
1 TABLESPOON FINELY CHOPPED
   SHALLOT
KOSHER SALT
FRESHLY GROUND BLACK PEPPER
2 TABLESPOONS CAPERS

4 TABLESPOONS EXTRA-VIRGIN
   OLIVE OIL
1 1/2 POUNDS DIVER SCALLOPS, TOUGH
   MUSCLE REMOVED FROM THE SIDE OF
   EACH SCALLOP, IF NECESSARY
1/4 CUP FINELY CHOPPED CHIVES

### TO COOK THE CAULIFLOWER

Pour 5 cups of the chicken stock into a medium saucepan over high heat, add the saffron, and bring to a boil. (If you prefer, you can use water here, but the cauliflower will have less flavor.) Decrease the heat to medium, add the cauliflower florets, and cook until just tender, 2 to 3 minutes. Using a slotted spoon, remove the cauliflower and set aside.

### TO BROWN THE BUTTER

Melt the 4 tablespoons butter in a medium skillet over medium heat, and continue cooking until it begins to turn brown, 7 to 8 minutes. You will see some black solids begin to form; at that point, remove the pan from the heat. Set the butter aside until cool; then strain it through a fine strainer to remove the black solids. Or if you prefer, taste the solids—if they have not burned, they will have a very concentrated nutty flavor and can be left in the vinaigrette.

### TO MAKE THE VINAIGRETTE

Heat the remaining 2 cups chicken stock in a large skillet over high heat and allow it to reduce by about three fourths, to 1/2 cup. Set aside to cool slightly. Put the stock, mustard, lemon juice, and shallot in a blender and, with the motor running, slowly pour in the browned butter in a steady stream. Or put the mustard in a medium nonreactive bowl and whisk in the reduced chicken stock, lemon juice, and shallot. Slowly add the brown butter in a steady stream while whisking. Season with salt and pepper, and stir in the capers.

### TO BROWN THE CAULIFLOWER

Heat 2 tablespoons of the olive oil in a large skillet over medium-high heat and cook the cauliflower, cut-side down, until lightly browned, 5 to 6 minutes (without turning). Remove the cauliflower to a plate and cover lightly to keep warm. Wipe out the skillet with paper towels.

### TO COOK THE SCALLOPS

Heat the remaining 2 tablespoons olive oil with the remaining 1 tablespoon butter in the same skillet over high heat. Season the scallops with salt and pepper. Decrease the heat to medium-high and cook the scallops until lightly golden, about 3 minutes per side.

### TO SERVE

Divide the scallops and cauliflower florets, browned-side up, among 4 warmed plates. Spoon the vinaigrette over both, and sprinkle with chopped chives.

# BACON-WRAPPED SHRIMP
## WITH AVOCADO, LIME, AND TOMATO JAM

SERVES 4 AS A FIRST COURSE / Think of this as a reconstructed version of that old favorite, Cobb salad. Its creation was inspired by the Cobb flavors—avocado, bacon, and tomato—but shrimp gives it a refreshing twist. You might also make it with large diver scallops. | Tomato jam is easy to make, and you can multiply the recipe. Use it as a condiment on grilled meats, fish, and seafood, in sandwiches, or with meatloaf.

### TOMATO JAM

1 (28-OUNCE) CAN PLUM TOMATOES, DRAINED (DISCARD THE JUICE OR SAVE FOR ANOTHER USE)

2 TABLESPOONS GRAPESEED OIL OR OTHER NEUTRAL OIL, SUCH AS CANOLA

2 TABLESPOONS FINELY CHOPPED PEELED FRESH GINGER

1 MEDIUM RED ONION, FINELY CHOPPED

1/2 CUP RED WINE VINEGAR

1/2 CUP PACKED BROWN SUGAR

1 TEASPOON DRIED HOT RED PEPPER FLAKES

1 TEASPOON KOSHER SALT

1 TABLESPOON HONEY

### SHRIMP

12 SLICES BACON, PREFERABLY NIMAN RANCH (SEE SOURCES)

12 JUMBO SHRIMP (ABOUT 1 1/4 POUNDS), PEELED AND DEVEINED, TAILS LEFT ON

2 RIPE HASS AVOCADOS

7 TABLESPOONS FRESHLY SQUEEZED LIME JUICE

KOSHER SALT

FRESHLY GROUND BLACK PEPPER

2 TABLESPOONS FINELY CHOPPED CHIVES

4 TEASPOONS EXTRA-VIRGIN OLIVE OIL

1/4 CUP LOOSELY PACKED CILANTRO LEAVES

### TO MAKE THE TOMATO JAM

Purée half the tomatoes in a food processor or blender. Crush the remaining tomatoes with your hands.

In a medium saucepan, heat the oil over medium-high heat and cook the ginger and onion, stirring, until the onion is soft, about 5 minutes. Add the vinegar, brown sugar, and pepper flakes and cook until the sugar is dissolved, about 3 minutes. Add both the crushed and puréed tomatoes and the salt, and bring to a boil. Decrease the heat to medium-low and cook, stirring occasionally, until reduced by half and thickened to a jam consistency, 35 to 40 minutes. Add the honey and set aside to cool. You will have about 1 1/2 cups, more than you need for this dish; save the remainder for another use. It can be refrigerated in an airtight container for up to 1 week.

### TO MAKE THE SHRIMP

Wrap 1 slice of bacon around each shrimp, beginning at the head of the shrimp and wrapping toward the tail (it will adhere). Heat a large skillet over medium heat and cook the shrimp until golden brown and cooked through, about 5 minutes on each side. Pour out any excess fat. Using tongs, remove the shrimp from the skillet and drain on paper towels.

While the shrimp are cooking, peel and pit the avocados (see page 40) and cut into a large dice. Place the avocados in a nonreactive bowl and toss very gently with 3 tablespoons of the lime juice. Season with salt and pepper, add the chives, and toss gently again.

### TO SERVE

Place a mound of avocado on each plate, and arrange the shrimp on top. Top each shrimp with about 1/2 teaspoon of the tomato jam. Drizzle with the olive oil, then with the remaining 4 tablespoons lime juice, and garnish with cilantro leaves.

# CRAB CAKES
## WITH LEMONY RÉMOULADE

SERVES 4 / A coating of crisp panko bread crumbs and the traditional spices in Old Bay Seasoning enhance the flavor and texture of fresh crabmeat in this classic recipe. Lemony rémoulade dresses them up a bit, but you can also try serving these crab cakes with Tomato Jam (page 73) for a spicier dish.

### LEMONY RÉMOULADE

1 CUP MAYONNAISE

2 TABLESPOONS FINELY CHOPPED CAPERS

2 TABLESPOONS FINELY CHOPPED CORNICHONS

1 TABLESPOON FINELY CHOPPED SHALLOT

1 TABLESPOON FINELY CHOPPED TARRAGON

GRATED ZEST OF 2 LEMONS

3 TABLESPOONS FRESHLY SQUEEZED LEMON JUICE, PLUS MORE IF NECESSARY

KOSHER SALT

FRESHLY GROUND BLACK PEPPER

### CRAB CAKES

2 TABLESPOONS BUTTER

2 RIBS CELERY, MINCED

3 SCALLIONS, THINLY SLICED (WHITE AND ABOUT 3 INCHES OF GREEN)

1 POUND LUMP CRABMEAT, PICKED OVER FOR SHELL FRAGMENTS

1 1/2 TEASPOONS OLD BAY SEASONING (SEE SOURCES)

2 TABLESPOONS FINE DRY BREAD CRUMBS

1/4 CUP MAYONNAISE

KOSHER SALT

FRESHLY GROUND BLACK PEPPER

1 EGG, LIGHTLY BEATEN

2 CUPS PANKO CRUMBS (SEE SOURCES)

ABOUT 1/4 CUP GRAPESEED OIL OR OTHER NEUTRAL OIL, SUCH AS CANOLA

1/4 CUP CHOPPED CHIVES

### TO MAKE THE RÉMOULADE

In a medium nonreactive bowl, combine the mayonnaise, capers, cornichons, shallot, tarragon, lemon zest and juice, and season with salt and pepper. Thin the sauce with additional lemon juice if necessary. You will have 1 1/2 cups—more than you need for this dish; save the remainder for another use. The rémoulade can be made ahead and refrigerated for up to 24 hours.

### TO MAKE THE CRAB CAKES

In a medium skillet over medium heat, melt the butter and sweat the celery and scallions until softened, about 5 minutes. Remove from the heat and allow to cool.

In a large mixing bowl, gently combine the crabmeat, scallions, celery mixture, Old Bay Seasoning, bread crumbs, and mayonnaise, being careful not to break up the lumps of crabmeat too much. Season with salt and pepper. Fold in the egg with a rubber spatula until just combined. Form into 8 to 10 cakes about 3 inches in diameter and 1/2 inch thick.

Refrigerate on a baking sheet or platter lined with waxed paper for at least 30 minutes but no more than 24 hours.

Place the panko crumbs in a deep plate or shallow bowl. Coat each crab cake with the crumbs and set aside.

Starting with half of the oil in a skillet over medium-high heat, fry the crab cakes in batches, about 3 minutes on each side. Use more oil as needed.

### TO SERVE

Place 2 crab cakes each on 4 plates, drizzle with the rémoulade, and garnish with the chopped chives.

# SEARED SEA BASS

## WITH ANISE, PISTACHIOS, AND MEYER LEMON PURÉE

SERVES 4 / Sea bass is a delicate fish that works best with a subtle accompaniment, and the Mediterranean flavors of anise, pistachio, and lemon are its perfect match. The crisp crust provides a textural contrast to the silken purée of Meyer lemons. | Made with my favorite lemons, this purée is a versatile condiment, relatively easy to make, tart, and delicious. Try it with poultry, vegetables, or rice, as well as with fish.

### MEYER LEMON PURÉE

1 POUND MEYER LEMONS (ABOUT
    5 MEDIUM; SEE NOTE AND SOURCES)

2 TABLESPOONS SUGAR

2 TABLESPOONS WATER

1/4 CUP EXTRA-VIRGIN OLIVE OIL

KOSHER SALT

1/4 CUP HONEY

### SEA BASS

2 TABLESPOONS OLIVE OIL

4 SEA BASS FILLETS, 6 TO 7 OUNCES
    EACH, SKIN REMOVED
    (THE FISHMONGER CAN DO THIS)

KOSHER SALT

FRESHLY GROUND BLACK PEPPER

1 TABLESPOON ANISEED

1/3 CUP PISTACHIO NUTS, TOASTED
    (PAGE 18) AND COARSELY CHOPPED

### TO MAKE THE LEMON PURÉE

Using a vegetable peeler, peel the zest from the lemons. Lay the pieces of zest flat and gently cut away the white pith with a small paring knife, holding the knife blade almost parallel to the work surface.

Bring a small saucepan of water to a boil, and boil the zest for 5 minutes. Drain and reserve.

With a small, sharp knife, cut away the white pith from the whole lemons. Quarter and seed the lemons, and put them in a small bowl with any juices.

In a blender, process the lemons, lemon zest, sugar, and 2 tablespoons water until puréed. With the motor running, slowly add the oil. Season with salt. You will have about 2 cups. The extra purée can be refrigerated in an airtight container for up to 1 week.

In a small bowl, whisk together 3/4 cup of the lemon purée and the honey, and set aside.

### TO SEAR THE SEA BASS

Heat the olive oil in a large skillet over medium-high heat. Season both sides of the fish with salt and pepper and press the aniseed into one side of the fish. Sear the seeded side for 4 to 5 minutes. Flip the fish and gently press the chopped pistachios over the aniseed. Continue searing for another 3 to 4 minutes, or until the fish is cooked through.

### TO SERVE

Place the fillets on 4 warmed plates. Spoon the lemon purée and honey mixture around the fish.

### NOTE

For the Meyer lemons, you may substitute 4 small regular lemons (about 3/4 pound) plus 1 medium orange. Use only half of the orange to start, then add more to the blender if the purée is too tart.

# SEARED TUNA
## WITH GINGER DRESSING

SERVES 4 / The most beautiful, most intensely colored tuna I have ever seen inspired this recipe. I cook it until it is just seared on the outside but still bright pink inside and serve it with refreshing tender greens. The tart, spicy, and sweet flavors are in the dressing rather than cooked with the tuna, so they serve as an accent to the fresh, pure flavor of the fish. | This versatile dressing is also delicious spooned over grilled or seared chicken or beef. You can use less oil, or even no oil, if you wish, to make it even more potent.

### GINGER DRESSING

2/3 CUP FRESHLY SQUEEZED LIME JUICE

1/3 CUP TAMARI SOY SAUCE

1/4 CUP HONEY

1/2 CUP EXTRA-VIRGIN OLIVE OIL

1/2 CUP FINELY CHOPPED PEELED FRESH
   GINGER

3 SCALLIONS, WHITE AND ABOUT
   3 INCHES OF GREEN, THINLY SLICED
   AND THEN COARSELY CHOPPED

1/2 TEASPOON FINELY MINCED JALAPEÑO,
   OR TO TASTE, OR SUBSTITUTE
   1/4 TEASPOON RED CHILE POWDER

1 CUP LOOSELY PACKED CILANTRO
   LEAVES

KOSHER SALT

FRESHLY GROUND BLACK PEPPER

### TUNA

2 TABLESPOONS EXTRA-VIRGIN
   OLIVE OIL

4 TUNA STEAKS, 5 TO 7 OUNCES EACH,
   3/4 TO 1 INCH THICK

KOSHER SALT

FRESHLY GROUND BLACK PEPPER

8 OUNCES ARUGULA, BABY ARUGULA,
   OR WATERCRESS

1/4 CUP PINE NUTS, TOASTED (PAGE 18)
   AND COARSELY CHOPPED

### TO MAKE THE DRESSING

In a medium nonreactive bowl, whisk together the lime juice, tamari soy sauce, honey, olive oil, ginger, scallions, jalapeño, and half of the cilantro leaves. Season to taste with salt and pepper.

### TO SEAR THE TUNA

Heat the olive oil over medium-high heat in one large or two medium skillets until hot but not smoking. Season the tuna with salt and pepper. Sear the tuna for 1 to 2 minutes per side for rare, or 3 minutes or longer to cook through, depending on thickness.

### TO SERVE

Cut each tuna steak into slices about 1/2 inch thick. In a medium bowl, toss the greens with a few tablespoons of the dressing. Divide the greens among four 4 plates and arrange the tuna slices on top. Spoon the remaining dressing over the tuna and garnish with the remaining 1/2 cup cilantro. Sprinkle with the pine nuts.

# CHICKEN GLAZED
## WITH HONEY, LIME, AND CHILE

SERVES 4 / This dish is inspired by *agrodolce* (an Italian word, but a universal concept)—the classic combination of sweet and sour. The careful balance of flavors heightens the excitement of chicken, which otherwise can be somewhat plain. You can spread the ginger and rosemary mixture on the chicken ahead of time, but don't cook it until the last minute. | Leftovers are great for sandwiches or chicken salad.

1/4 CUP HONEY

2 TABLESPOONS FRESHLY SQUEEZED LIME JUICE

1/2 TEASPOON RED CHILE POWDER

2 TABLESPOONS MINCED PEELED FRESH GINGER

1 TABLESPOON PLUS 1 TEASPOON FINELY CHOPPED ROSEMARY

1 1/2 TABLESPOONS GRATED LIME ZEST

4 TABLESPOONS EXTRA-VIRGIN OLIVE OIL

KOSHER SALT

FRESHLY GROUND BLACK PEPPER

4 WHOLE CHICKEN BREASTS, SKIN ON AND PART OF WING ATTACHED

4 THIN SLICES LIME (OPTIONAL)

In a small nonreactive bowl, combine the honey, lime juice, and 1/4 teaspoon of the chile powder and set aside.

In a small bowl, combine the ginger, rosemary, lime zest, remaining 1/4 teaspoon chile powder, 2 tablespoons of the olive oil, 1/2 teaspoon salt, and 1/4 teaspoon pepper.

Starting at one side of each chicken breast, gently slide your fingers under the skin, loosening it but leaving it attached at one side. Spread the ginger and rosemary mixture under the skin. Season the chicken breasts with salt and pepper.

Heat the remaining 2 tablespoons olive oil in a large skillet over high heat until the oil is hot but not smoking. Place the chicken breasts in the pan, skin-side down. (Use two skillets if necessary, to avoid crowding.) Decrease the heat to medium-high and cook until browned, 8 to 9 minutes. Turn the chicken pieces over and cook the other side until browned, 8 to 9 minutes. The chicken should be almost cooked through.

Begin brushing the chicken generously with the honey-lime mixture. Cook for another 1 to 3 minutes, turning the chicken over and brushing both sides. Do not begin brushing it earlier in the cooking process, or the honey will burn.

When the chicken is cooked through, baste again just before serving. Garnish with the lime slices, if desired.

# DUCK BREAST
## WITH POMEGRANATE BASTE

SERVES 4 / Duck and pomegranate work beautifully together. Pomegranate molasses adds an even more intense fruit flavor than plain juice would provide and goes well with both duck and fresh herbs. | Try to use muscovy duck, if available. It is much leaner than its Long Island cousins.

### GLAZE AND SAUCE

$2/3$ CUP POMEGRANATE MOLASSES
    (SEE SOURCES)
$2/3$ CUP RED WINE VINEGAR
$1/4$ CUP HONEY
2 CUPS BROWN CHICKEN STOCK OR
    VEAL STOCK, REDUCED TO $1/2$ CUP,
    OR USE $1/2$ CUP DEMI-GLACE (SEE
    SOURCES)

### DUCK

4 DUCK BREASTS, PREFERABLY MUSCOVY
    (SEE SOURCES)
KOSHER SALT
FRESHLY GROUND BLACK PEPPER

2 ORANGES
1 TABLESPOON EXTRA-VIRGIN OLIVE OIL
2 TABLESPOONS BUTTER
1 LARGE OR 2 SMALL BULBS FENNEL,
    CORED AND CUT INTO PIECES ABOUT
    $1/4$ INCH THICK
$1/2$ CUP POMEGRANATE SEEDS
    (OPTIONAL)

### TO MAKE THE POMEGRANATE GLAZE

Combine the pomegranate molasses and vinegar in a small saucepan over high heat. When it comes to a boil, decrease the heat to medium and add the honey. Simmer until reduced by about half.

### TO MAKE THE POMEGRANATE SAUCE

Combine half of the pomegranate glaze and the reduced stock in a small saucepan over medium-low heat, and keep warm.

### TO SAUTÉ THE DUCK

Place a large skillet over medium-high heat until hot. Score the duck skin lightly in a crosshatch pattern; do not cut through the flesh. Season both sides of the breasts with salt and pepper, place skin-side down in the hot skillet (be careful not to crowd them, or use two pans), and cook until nicely browned, 7 to 8 minutes. Flip the breasts and cook for another 3 to 5 minutes for medium-rare. Brush generously on both sides with the reserved pomegranate glaze, and set aside to rest, tented with foil, for 5 minutes.

### TO PREPARE THE ORANGE AND FENNEL

Peel the oranges as close as possible to the flesh, cut the fruit free from the membranes, and reserve in a small bowl.

Heat the olive oil and 1 tablespoon of the butter in a large skillet over medium-high heat. Add the fennel, decrease the heat to medium-low, and sauté gently for about 5 minutes, without browning the fennel. Season with salt and pepper. Add the orange sections and toss to heat through.

Bring the reserved pomegranate sauce to a simmer, stir in the remaining butter, and remove from the heat. Season with salt and pepper.

### TO SERVE

Cut the duck breasts into quarter-inch slices. Divide the fennel and orange sections among 4 warmed plates, and fan the duck slices alongside. Pour the sauce around the duck, and sprinkle with pomegranate seeds, if desired.

# SPICY SOY-GLAZED
# BEEF FILET WITH SHIITAKES AND BOK CHOY

SERVES 4 / Many of my favorite beef dishes are Thai or Vietnamese, and this recipe is inspired by those cuisines. It's lighter than most Western beef preparations, and the soy, chile, and sesame oil give it exotic flavors. Soy-Glazed Beef is flavorful enough that it does not need an additional sauce, and it pairs well with sweet, aromatic Coconut Basmati Rice (page 93).

2 CUPS MIRIN (SWEET JAPANESE RICE WINE; SEE SOURCES)

1/2 CUP LOW-SODIUM SOY SAUCE

1/4 CUP ASIAN SESAME OIL

1/4 CUP HONEY

2 TABLESPOONS MINCED PEELED FRESH GINGER

6 SCALLIONS, COARSELY CHOPPED

4 WHOLE STAR ANISE, BROKEN INTO PIECES

1 TABLESPOON MINCED FRESH RED CHILE, OR 1 TEASPOON DRIED HOT RED PEPPER FLAKES

1 SMALL BUNCH CILANTRO (ABOUT 8 SPRIGS)

1 1/2 POUNDS BEEF TENDERLOIN, CUT CROSSWISE INTO 1-INCH-THICK SLICES

8 OUNCES FRESH SHIITAKE MUSHROOMS, STEMS REMOVED AND CAPS THICKLY SLICED

3 TABLESPOONS EXTRA-VIRGIN OLIVE OIL

FRESHLY GROUND BLACK PEPPER

ABOUT 6 CUPS BABY BOK CHOY, QUARTERED LENGTHWISE, OR BOK CHOY, CUT INTO 2-INCH LENGTHS

In a large nonreactive bowl, combine the mirin, soy sauce, sesame oil, honey, ginger, scallions, star anise, chile, and half of the cilantro sprigs. Strain 1/2 cup of the marinade, and set aside.

Place the beef slices in one layer in a large, shallow pan or dish. Add the mushrooms to the beef and cover both with the remaining marinade, making sure they are well coated. Cover and refrigerate for 1/2 hour, turn the slices over, and refrigerate for another 1/2 hour.

Heat 2 tablespoons of the olive oil in a large skillet over medium-high heat. Remove the beef from the marinade, blot off the excess with paper towels, and season with pepper (the marinade contains plenty of salt). Cook the slices for about 3 minutes per side for medium-rare. About 1 minute before removing the beef from the pan, brush it with about 1/4 cup of the reserved marinade. Remove the meat from the pan, and allow it to rest for 5 minutes.

Heat the remaining tablespoon of olive oil in a medium skillet over medium-high heat and sauté the mushrooms and bok choy for 2 to 3 minutes. Add the remaining marinade (you should have about 1/4 cup), and simmer until the mushrooms and bok choy are cooked through, about 5 minutes. Season with pepper.

To serve, divide the mushrooms and bok choy among 4 plates. Halve each piece of beef crosswise (the slices will now be 1/2 inch thick) and fan the slices, alternating cut sides with browned sides, alongside the mushrooms and bok choy. Garnish with the remaining 4 cilantro sprigs.

# PAN-CRISPED GOAT CHEESE WITH FIGS AND ARUGULA

SERVES 4 / After tasting goat cheese warmed and slightly softened, it will be hard for you to eat it any other way. The cheese melts in your mouth and is especially delicious with something sweet, such as fresh figs, and something crunchy, such as sourdough toast. This makes a simple, colorful first course before any roasted chicken or meat main dish.

1 LOG (6 OUNCES) SOFT, FRESH GOAT CHEESE

1 CUP PANKO CRUMBS (SEE SOURCES) OR SUBSTITUTE FRESH WHITE BREAD CRUMBS

KOSHER SALT

1 EGG, LIGHTLY BEATEN

2 BUNCHES ARUGULA, TOUGH STEMS REMOVED

6 FRESH FIGS, TRIMMED AND HALVED

1 TABLESPOON AGED BALSAMIC VINEGAR, PLUS MORE FOR DRIZZLING

4 TABLESPOONS EXTRA-VIRGIN OLIVE OIL

1/2 TEASPOON FRESHLY SQUEEZED LEMON JUICE

FRESHLY GROUND PEPPER

1/2 SOURDOUGH OR PLAIN BAGUETTE, THINLY SLICED AT A SHARP ANGLE AND LIGHTLY TOASTED

Cut the goat cheese crosswise into eight 1/2-inch-thick rounds. To cut through the cheese smoothly, run the knife under very hot water before each cut, wiping the excess cheese from the blade each time. Or use a long piece of dental floss and, holding it taut, pull the floss down through the cheese to make slices (this is the easier way).

Combine the panko crumbs with 1 teaspoon salt in a shallow bowl and set aside. Place the beaten egg in a separate shallow bowl. Dip each goat cheese round in the beaten egg, then in the panko mixture, coating completely. Refrigerate the cheese slices, covered with plastic, for at least 30 minutes or up to 1 day.

In a medium bowl, gently toss the arugula and the figs with the 1 tablespoon balsamic vinegar, 2 tablespoons of the olive oil, and the lemon juice and season with salt and pepper. Divide the arugula among 4 plates. Arrange 3 fig halves around the arugula on each plate, cut-sides facing outward.

Heat the remaining 2 tablespoons olive oil in a large skillet over medium heat and sauté the cheese rounds until golden brown, about 1 minute per side. Arrange the cheese rounds on top of the arugula. Drizzle with additional balsamic vinegar, if desired, and serve with the sourdough toasts.

# PINEAPPLE AND RHUBARB WITH BROWN SUGAR AND BASIL

SERVES 4 / This light dessert is easy to prepare and welcome after a robust meal. Ripe, golden pineapple and rosy rhubarb look beautiful together and combine sweetness and citric sharpness, and fresh basil adds an unexpected herbal flavor.

4 TABLESPOONS (1/2 STICK) BUTTER

1/2 LARGE OR 1 SMALL PINEAPPLE, CUT INTO PIECES ABOUT 1/2 INCH THICK

1/2 POUND RHUBARB (ABOUT 2 LARGE, WIDE STALKS OR 3 TO 4 THINNER STALKS), CUT DIAGONALLY INTO PIECES ABOUT 1/2 INCH THICK

1 CUP MUSCAT OR OTHER SWEET WHITE WINE

6 TABLESPOONS LIGHT BROWN SUGAR

1/4 TEASPOON GROUND CINNAMON

1 VANILLA BEAN, SPLIT LENGTHWISE

4 LARGE BASIL LEAVES, CUT INTO THIN RIBBONS

In a large skillet over medium-high heat, melt the butter and cook the pineapple until lightly browned, 2 to 3 minutes. Flip the pineapple pieces and, after about another minute, add the rhubarb. Cook for another 1 to 2 minutes (be careful not to cook the rhubarb too long or it will become mushy) and add the muscat, brown sugar, and cinnamon. Scrape the seeds from the vanilla bean into the pan, discarding the pod or saving it for another use. Stir to dissolve the sugar and cook for another 2 to 3 minutes.

To serve, divide the pineapple and rhubarb among 4 plates. Spoon the sauce over them, and top with the basil.

### VARIATION

Substitute 1 pint of strawberries for the rhubarb. Halve the large berries and leave the small ones whole.

# CARAMELIZED
# MANGO WITH LIME AND BLUEBERRIES

**SERVES 4 /** Mango and lime—perfect sweet and tart partners—here are warmed and glazed with brown sugar. Juicy blueberries add freshness and color.

2 TABLESPOONS BUTTER

1/4 CUP LIGHT BROWN SUGAR

2 RIPE MANGOES, PEELED AND CUT INTO
   1/4-INCH SLICES

2 TEASPOONS GRATED LIME ZEST

JUICE OF 1 LIME

1 CUP BLUEBERRIES

Melt the butter in a medium skillet over medium-high heat, add the brown sugar, and stir to dissolve, about 1 minute. Add the mango slices and cook for 2 to 3 minutes, tossing to coat with the butter-sugar mixture. Add the lime zest, lime juice, and blueberries and toss to coat.

To serve, divide among 4 plates and drizzle with the sauce from the pan.

### VARIATIONS

Substitute an equal amount of papaya or pineapple for the mango. Or, add 1/4 cup chopped toasted macadamia nuts to the pan with the blueberries.

# CHERRIES SAUTÉED
# IN PINOT NOIR WITH CRÈME FRAÎCHE

**SERVES 4 /** Here is a simple but decadant summer dessert. It is pretty served ungarnished in beautiful shallow bowls—preferably white, to show off the deep red color of the reduced wine. Make it with only the best ripe, sweet cherries. | You can also spoon the sautéed cherries over vanilla ice cream for a more casual dessert, or around slices of your favorite pound cake.

2 CUPS PINOT NOIR
1/2 CUP PLUS 1 TABLESPOON SUGAR
1/2 CUP CRÈME FRAÎCHE (SEE NOTE)
1 TABLESPOON BUTTER
1 POUND SWEET CHERRIES, PITTED
1/2 VANILLA BEAN, SPLIT LENGTHWISE
PINCH OF SALT

In a medium saucepan over medium-high heat, bring the pinot noir and 1/2 cup of the sugar to a boil. Decrease the heat to medium-low and simmer until reduced by half, 20 to 30 minutes. (You can make this ahead and refrigerate it in an airtight container for up to 1 week.)

In a small bowl, combine the crème fraîche with the remaining 1 tablespoon sugar, and stir until smooth.

In a medium sauté pan over medium-high heat, melt the butter and sauté the cherries for 30 seconds to 1 minute; then add the pinot noir reduction. Add the vanilla bean to the cherries, scraping some of the seeds out into the pan first. Add the salt and continue cooking, tossing the cherries occasionally, for about 5 minutes. Discard the vanilla bean.

To serve, spoon the cherries into the center of 4 shallow bowls and pour the liquid over them. Drizzle the crème fraîche around the cherries into the liquid. Serve immediately, moving the bowls gently to the table, so as not to disturb the pattern of the crème fraîche in the liquid.

NOTE

To make 1 cup crème fraîche, combine 1 cup heavy cream with 2 tablespoons sour cream or buttermilk in a glass bowl or container and cover tightly. Let stand at room temperature until thick, from 8 to 24 hours. Stir when thickened. Can be refrigerated for up to 1 week.

CHAPTER 4/ FROM THE TERRACE

# FROM THE TERRACE

Fortunate are the city-dwellers who have a terrace or backyard. This chapter is for them and for home chefs everywhere who love to cook alfresco. But even if you are not blessed with an outdoor grill, all is not lost: Every one of the dishes in this chapter can be adapted to a skillet or grill pan. When adapting grill recipes to pan cooking, follow these simple rules:

1 / Sauté in olive oil or grapeseed oil (the latter has a neutral flavor and high smoking point).

2 / Cook over high or medium-high heat.

3 / Cook for approximately the same time as you would on the grill, but check frequently for doneness and adjust the timing to your taste.

You may want to try an indoor electric grill, either one that is open or one with a hinged cover that contains grids, allowing the food to cook on both sides at once. When you use these, marinated foods should be patted dry before grilling and any glaze should be added only during the last few minutes of cooking. If your food is seared at a high enough temperature, the results come fairly close to outdoor grilling.

One great thing about grilling is that you can season or marinate the food ahead of time and then, when you are ready, fire up the grill and cook. Although many of the dishes in this chapter receive this flavor-enhancing treatment, marination times vary with the delicacy of the food: Grilled Swordfish with Green Olive Tapenade (page 94) will need less marinating time than Brochette of Lamb with Honey-Lime Marinade (page 98). Charred Vegetables with Orange Blossom Honey and Pecorino (page 92) and Lime and Honey Glazed Eggplant with Mint Chutney (page 90) can simply be brushed with olive oil and seasoned a few minutes in advance and then brushed with glaze as they cook.

As with sautéing, it is best to let the food sit over the heat long enough to brown before you turn it. Cover the food if it will cook for a long time, but don't bother covering it for a short stay on the grill.

# LIME AND HONEY
# GLAZED EGGPLANT
## WITH MINT CHUTNEY

*SERVES 4 /* Slices of eggplant, preferably the long, purple Japanese variety, are delicious grilled and need only a brushing with oil and honey. Served with an Indian-style chutney made with orange juice, toasted pine nuts, and fresh mint, the combination is flavorful and refreshing.

### MINT CHUTNEY

3 CUPS FRESHLY SQUEEZED ORANGE
    JUICE

3 TABLESPOONS PINE NUTS, TOASTED
    (PAGE 18) AND COARSELY CHOPPED

1/3 CUP LOOSELY PACKED MINT LEAVES,
    CUT INTO FINE RIBBONS

1/4 CUP PLUS 2 TEASPOONS EXTRA-
    VIRGIN OLIVE OIL

FLEUR DE SEL, COARSE SEA SALT, OR
    KOSHER SALT

FRESHLY GROUND BLACK PEPPER

1/4 CUP HONEY

1/4 CUP FRESHLY SQUEEZED LIME JUICE

4 TO 6 JAPANESE EGGPLANTS, OR
    2 MEDIUM GLOBE EGGPLANTS

### TO MAKE THE MINT CHUTNEY

In a medium saucepan over high heat, bring the orange juice to a boil. Decrease the heat to medium and boil until reduced to about 1/2 cup, 30 to 40 minutes. Set aside to cool.

In a small bowl, combine the pine nuts, mint, reduced orange juice, and 1 teaspoon of the olive oil. Stir to combine and season with salt and pepper. Set aside.

### TO GRILL THE EGGPLANT

In a small bowl, combine 1/4 cup of the olive oil, the honey, and lime juice and set aside.

Light a medium-hot fire in the grill.

Slice the eggplants 1/4 to 1/3 inch thick, lengthwise if using Japanese eggplants and crosswise if using globe eggplants. Brush the slices with the remaining teaspoon of olive oil, season with salt, and grill for 1 to 2 minutes, rotating once about 45 degrees to achieve crosshatch grill marks. Flip the slices, brush with the oil and honey mixture, and grill for 1 to 2 minutes on the second side, rotating once. Remove the eggplant slices from the grill and arrange on a platter or 4 individual plates. Brush again with the oil and honey mixture, and top with mint chutney. Season lightly with pepper.

# CHARRED VEGETABLES
## WITH ORANGE BLOSSOM HONEY AND PECORINO

SERVES 4 AS A FIRST COURSE OR SIDE DISH / Here is a new take on an old favorite, inspired by a dish that one of our chefs discovered in Sicily. Orange-flavored honey makes a perfect glaze when brushed on at the end of grilling (watch carefully so it doesn't burn). Not only does the honey enhance the flavor, it helps caramelize the vegetables by bringing out their natural sugars. Pecorino and honey are my favorite Tuscan combination, enhancing both vegetables and fruits (see Pears with Honey, Walnut Toast, and Pecorino, page 55).

1/2 CUP ORANGE BLOSSOM HONEY (SEE SOURCES), OR SUBSTITUTE REGULAR HONEY MIXED WITH 1/4 CUP FRESH ORANGE JUICE

1/2 CUP EXTRA-VIRGIN OLIVE OIL, PLUS ADDITIONAL FOR BRUSHING VEGETABLES

2 MEDIUM ZUCCHINI, SLICED LENGTH-WISE 1/4 INCH THICK

2 MEDIUM YELLOW SQUASH, SLICED LENGTHWISE 1/4 INCH THICK

2 SMALL JAPANESE EGGPLANTS, SLICED LENGTHWISE 1/4 INCH THICK

8 OUNCES FRESH SHIITAKE MUSHROOMS, STEMS REMOVED AND CAPS THICKLY SLICED

1 MEDIUM BULB FENNEL, SLICED 1/4 INCH THICK

12 MEDIUM SPEARS ASPARAGUS, ENDS TRIMMED (ABOUT 3/4 POUND; SEE NOTE)

FLEUR DE SEL, COARSE SEA SALT, OR KOSHER SALT

FRESHLY GROUND BLACK PEPPER

2 OUNCES PECORINO TOSCANO CHEESE (SEE SOURCES), SHAVED OR THINLY SLICED

16 TO 20 BASIL LEAVES, COARSELY TORN

Light a medium-hot fire in the grill.

In a medium nonreactive bowl, whisk the honey with the 1/2 cup olive oil to thoroughly combine.

Brush both sides of all of the vegetables with olive oil and season with salt. Grill until nicely charred, about 1 minute. (If using very thin asparagus spears, add these to the grill last, as they will cook quickly.) Using tongs, flip all of the vegetables over and brush with the oil and honey mixture. When the second side has charred, after about 1 minute, remove the vegetables to a heated platter, flipping them over and brushing again with the oil and honey mixture.

To serve, arrange the vegetables on 4 warmed plates and season with freshly ground black pepper and salt, if desired. Top with pecorino shavings and torn basil leaves.

NOTE

If using very large asparagus spears, first blanch them for a minute or two in a large pot of boiling water and then plunge them into a bowl of ice water. Drain the asparagus, dry them on paper towels, and proceed with the recipe.

# RED CHILE BARBECUED SALMON

## WITH COCONUT BASMATI RICE

SERVES 4 / Because salmon is a fatty fish, it can stand up to intense, hot flavors, such as the ones in this spicy glaze. The spiciness of the glazed fish marries perfectly with basmati rice, an aromatic Indian grain with a nutlike flavor. | Cooking the rice with coconut milk gives it a creamy, velvety quality and a slightly sweet flavor. The rice is also great with Miso-Grilled Tuna with Savoy Cabbage (page 95) and with Spicy Soy-Glazed Beef Filet with Shiitakes and Bok Choy (page 80). | You can make the barbecue sauce up to 4 days ahead and refrigerate it in an airtight container. It will enhance grilled shrimp or chicken as well as salmon.

### BARBECUE SAUCE

1 CUP CANNED CRUSHED TOMATOES

1/2 CUP RED WINE VINEGAR

1/2 CUP BROWN SUGAR

1/2 MEDIUM RED ONION, COARSELY
   CHOPPED

2 TABLESPOONS COARSELY CHOPPED
   PEELED FRESH GINGER

2 TEASPOONS COARSELY CHOPPED
   CANNED CHIPOTLE PEPPER, OR USE
   DRIED CHILES TO TASTE

1 TABLESPOON PLUS 1 TEASPOON
   EXTRA-VIRGIN OLIVE OIL

KOSHER SALT

FRESHLY GROUND BLACK PEPPER

### COCONUT BASMATI RICE

2 CUPS BASMATI RICE

2 CUPS CANNED UNSWEETENED
   COCONUT MILK

2 CUPS WATER

KOSHER SALT

1/4 CUP COARSELY CHOPPED CILANTRO

### SALMON

4 SALMON FILLETS, 6 TO 7 OUNCES
   EACH, SKIN REMOVED

KOSHER SALT

FRESHLY GROUND BLACK PEPPER

### TO MAKE THE BARBECUE SAUCE

In a medium saucepan over medium-high heat, combine the crushed tomato, vinegar, brown sugar, onion, ginger, chipotle, olive oil, and 2 teaspoons salt. Bring to a boil, decrease the heat to medium-low, and simmer for 35 to 40 minutes. Purée in a blender or food processor and season to taste with salt and pepper. If desired, add more chipotle and process again. Pour into a medium bowl and reserve. Can be refrigerated for up to 4 days.

### TO MAKE THE RICE

In a medium saucepan over high heat (you can wash and reuse the barbecue sauce pan), combine the rice, coconut milk, water, and 1 teaspoon salt, and bring to a boil. Decrease the heat to low, cover, and simmer for 15 minutes. Remove from the heat, season to taste with salt, and stir in the chopped cilantro.

### TO GRILL THE SALMON

Light a medium-hot fire in the grill. Season the salmon with salt and pepper, and brush on both sides with the barbecue sauce. Grill for 3 to 4 minutes per side for medium-rare, brushing with the sauce while grilling. When the salmon is cooked, remove it from the grill and brush generously with additional sauce.

Serve the salmon with the rice.

# GRILLED SWORDFISH
## WITH GREEN OLIVE TAPENADE

SERVES 4 / For this creation, I was inspired by one of the first dishes I cooked early in my career, at Malvasia. It was a rustic, Sicilian-style combination of grilled fish with sautéed potatoes, tomatoes, garlic, and black olives. This subtler version is a bit more urban, without the assertive garlic and with a milder type of olives.

### TAPENADE

1 CUP PICHOLINE OLIVES, PITTED

2 TABLESPOONS PINE NUTS, TOASTED
(PAGE 18)

3 TABLESPOONS EXTRA-VIRGIN
OLIVE OIL

1 TABLESPOON WATER

1 TEASPOON FRESHLY SQUEEZED LEMON
JUICE

1/4 TEASPOON RED CHILE POWDER

KOSHER SALT

FRESHLY GROUND BLACK PEPPER

### SWORDFISH

4 SWORDFISH STEAKS, 6 TO 7 OUNCES
EACH

ABOUT 1/2 CUP EXTRA-VIRGIN OLIVE OIL

1 TEASPOON CAYENNE PEPPER

8 PLUM TOMATOES

1 POUND FINGERLING POTATOES,
UNPEELED, HALVED LENGTHWISE, OR
SUBSTITUTE RED BLISS POTATOES
CUT INTO 3/4-INCH SLICES

KOSHER SALT

FRESHLY GROUND BLACK PEPPER

8 SPRIGS ROSEMARY

JUICE OF 1 LEMON

GRATED ZEST OF 1 LEMON

### TO MAKE THE TAPENADE

Put the olives, pine nuts, olive oil, water, lemon juice, and chile powder in the bowl of a food processor or blender and process until smooth. Season with salt and pepper. You will have about 1 cup—more than you need; save the remainder for another use.

### TO PREPARE THE SWORDFISH AND ASSEMBLE THE DISH

Put the swordfish steaks in a shallow bowl, coat with some of the olive oil, and sprinkle lightly with cayenne. Cover with plastic wrap and refrigerate for 1/2 hour to 2 hours.

When you are ready to cook, light a medium-hot fire in the grill. Fill a large bowl with ice and water. Bring a large pot of salted water to a boil.

With a small, sharp knife, cut away the stem end of each tomato, and cut an X on the bottom end. Put the tomatoes in the boiling water for 1 to 2 minutes, remove with a slotted spoon, and plunge them into the ice water. (Keep the pot of boiling water on the stove.) Drain and peel the tomatoes (the skin will peel off easily), quarter them lengthwise, and remove the seeds.

Add the potatoes to the pot of boiling water and cook until slightly underdone, about 7 minutes. Drain the potatoes and place on a platter or baking sheet in one layer to cool.

Season the swordfish fillets with salt and pepper and grill 3 to 4 minutes per side, for medium-rare.

While the fish is grilling, heat 3 tablespoons of the olive oil in a large skillet over medium-high heat. Add the potatoes and 4 sprigs of the rosemary and cook until the potatoes are lightly browned, 1 to 2 minutes per side. Add the tomatoes and toss to warm through. Discard the rosemary sprigs.

Divide the potatoes and tomatoes among 4 warmed plates, arranging them in the center of each plate, and top with a swordfish fillet. Top each fillet with a dollop of the olive tapenade and drizzle with lemon juice. Garnish with the lemon zest and remaining rosemary sprigs.

# MISO-GRILLED
## TUNA WITH SAVOY CABBAGE

SERVES 4 / A savory miso glaze gives the tuna incredible caramelization and makes for beautiful grill marks, and the briefly braised savoy cabbage provides a crisp backdrop. Be sure to serve the tuna with the creamy Coconut Risotto Cakes (page 149), based on a risotto made with sake and finished with coconut milk, scallions, and ginger. These cakes are the perfect companion to the Asian flavors of the tuna. For a somewhat simpler accompaniment, try Coconut Basmati Rice (page 93).

**TUNA**

1/4 CUP MISO PASTE (SEE SOURCES)

1 CUP MIRIN (SWEET JAPANESE RICE WINE; SEE SOURCES)

1/2 CUP ASIAN SESAME OIL

1/2 CUP EXTRA-VIRGIN OLIVE OIL

1/2 CUP RICE WINE VINEGAR

3 TABLESPOONS COARSELY CHOPPED PEELED FRESH GINGER

5 SCALLIONS, WHITE AND ABOUT 3 INCHES OF GREEN, THINLY SLICED

4 TUNA STEAKS, 6 TO 7 OUNCES EACH, ABOUT 1 INCH THICK

**CABBAGE**

1 TABLESPOON EXTRA-VIRGIN OLIVE OIL

1 TEASPOON BUTTER

1 HEAD SAVOY CABBAGE, SLICED CROSSWISE ABOUT 1/2 INCH THICK

1/4 CUP CHICKEN STOCK, CANNED LOW-SODIUM BROTH, OR WATER

1 TEASPOON FRESHLY SQUEEZED LEMON JUICE

KOSHER SALT

FRESHLY GROUND BLACK PEPPER

COCONUT RISOTTO CAKES (PAGE 149) AS ACCOMPANIMENT

1/4 CUP BLACK SESAME SEEDS (OPTIONAL)

CILANTRO SPRIGS

**TO MAKE THE TUNA**

In a medium bowl, whisk together the miso paste, mirin, sesame oil, olive oil, rice wine vinegar, chopped ginger, and scallions. Set aside 1/2 cup of the marinade. Place the tuna steaks in a shallow dish, cover with the remaining marinade, and turn several times to coat. Cover and refrigerate for 1 to 2 hours.

**TO MAKE THE CABBAGE**

Just before you put the tuna on the grill, heat the olive oil and butter in a medium skillet over medium-high heat and add the sliced cabbage. Sauté for about 1 minute to wilt but not brown the cabbage. Add the chicken stock, and cook 4 to 5 minutes more. Add the lemon juice and season with salt and pepper. Cover and keep warm.

Light a medium-hot fire in the grill. Remove the tuna steaks from the marinade, season with pepper, and place on the grill. Cook 1 to 2 minutes per side for rare or 3 minutes per side for medium.

**TO SERVE**

Cut each tuna steak into 1/2-inch slices. Divide the tuna among 4 warmed plates and place the cabbage alongside. Place 1 Coconut Risotto Cake on each plate. Drizzle with the reserved marinade, and garnish with black sesame seeds, if desired, and cilantro sprigs.

# MOROCCAN SPICED
# SHRIMP WITH ARTICHOKES AND POMEGRANATE

SERVES 4 AS A FIRST COURSE / There is a lot going on in this beautiful dish. Smoky, spicy shrimp contrast with buttery artichokes, and pomegranate molasses brings the flavors and textures together. The two main elements are given special treatment, so that this becomes far more than just a shrimp dish with artichokes.

1 CUP PLUS 1 TABLESPOON EXTRA-
   VIRGIN OLIVE OIL, PLUS ADDITIONAL
   FOR COOKING ARTICHOKES

2 TEASPOONS GROUND CUMIN

2 TEASPOONS PAPRIKA

2 TEASPOONS GROUND GINGER

1 TEASPOON GROUND CARDAMOM

1 TEASPOON GROUND TURMERIC

1 TEASPOON RED CHILE POWDER

1 POUND LARGE SHRIMP (16 TO 20),
   PEELED AND DEVEINED, TAILS LEFT ON

4 LEMONS

4 LARGE ARTICHOKES

5 CLOVES GARLIC, PEELED

4 SPRIGS ROSEMARY

KOSHER SALT

FRESHLY GROUND BLACK PEPPER

4 CUPS LOOSELY PACKED BABY ARUGULA
   OR OTHER BABY GREENS

8 LARGE BASIL LEAVES, CUT INTO THIN
   RIBBONS

1/4 CUP POMEGRANATE MOLASSES
   (SEE SOURCES)

1/4 CUP POMEGRANATE SEEDS
   (OPTIONAL)

In a medium nonreactive bowl, combine 1 cup of the olive oil, the cumin, paprika, ginger, cardamom, turmeric, and chile powder. Add the shrimp and toss to coat. Cover with plastic wrap and refrigerate for 1 hour or up to 3 hours. About halfway through, toss the shrimp again to redistribute the marinade.

Halve the lemons, and squeeze the juice into a large non-reactive bowl, reserving 1 tablespoon of juice. Add the lemon halves to the bowl and fill with water. For each artichoke, first cut off the stem and then, starting at the base, snap off all of the tough outer leaves. Using a sharp paring knife, trim around the base until no dark green areas remain. Gently cut away and discard all of the tender leaves, leaving the heart. Using a small spoon, scoop out the choke. Place the artichoke hearts in the lemon water immediately, to prevent discoloration.

In a large skillet over medium heat, heat about 1 inch of olive oil. Decrease the heat to medium-low, add the artichoke hearts, garlic, and rosemary, and simmer gently, turning the artichoke hearts occasionally, until they are easily pierced with a knife, 20 to 30 minutes, depending on their size. Remove them from the oil using a slotted spoon, drain on paper towels, and cut them into quarters. The artichoke hearts can be refrigerated in their cooking oil, covered, for 1 to 3 days.

Light a medium-hot fire in the grill.

Remove the shrimp from the marinade, season with salt and pepper, and grill for 2 to 3 minutes per side, or until opaque. Brush the shrimp with the marinade while grilling.

In a medium nonreactive bowl, place the arugula leaves, artichoke hearts, half of the basil, 1 tablespoon oil, and the reserved 1 tablespoon of lemon juice. Toss to combine, and season with salt and pepper. Place a mound of arugula and 4 artichoke quarters in the center of each of 4 plates. Arrange the shrimp on top of the arugula, drizzle with pomegranate molasses, and garnish with the remaining basil leaves and pomegranate seeds, if desired.

# BROCHETTE OF LAMB WITH HONEY-LIME MARINADE

SERVES 4 / Yogurt tenderizes the lamb before grilling, and a touch of lime tames its robustness. This simple brochette treats you to the exotic flavors and aromas of cumin, tahini, and mint. Serve it with Couscous with Toasted Almonds and Cumin (page 162) for added texture and spice.

2 CUPS PLAIN YOGURT

2 TABLESPOONS EXTRA-VIRGIN OLIVE OIL

1/4 CUP HONEY

1/4 CUP PLUS 1 TABLESPOON FRESHLY SQUEEZED LIME JUICE

3/4 TEASPOON CAYENNE PEPPER

1/2 CUP TAHINI (SEE SOURCES)

1 TEASPOON GROUND CUMIN

KOSHER SALT

2 BONELESS LAMB LOINS, ABOUT 10 OUNCES EACH, CUT CROSSWISE INTO PIECES 1 INCH THICK (SEE SOURCES), OR HAVE YOUR BUTCHER DEBONE A FULL RACK OF LAMB TO GET THE SAME QUANTITY OF MEAT

FRESHLY GROUND BLACK PEPPER

COUSCOUS WITH TOASTED ALMONDS AND CUMIN (PAGE 162) AS ACCOMPANIMENT

1 SMALL BUNCH MINT (OR 16 TO 20 LARGE LEAVES), COARSELY TORN

In a medium nonreactive bowl, whisk together the yogurt, olive oil, honey, lime juice, cayenne, tahini, cumin, and 1 teaspoon salt. Place the lamb pieces in a large glass baking dish, cover with the marinade, and wrap tightly with plastic wrap. Refrigerate for 3 to 6 hours.

Light a medium-hot fire in the grill. If using wooden skewers, soak them in water for about 10 minutes.

Thread the lamb onto metal or wooden skewers and place on the grill. Brush with marinade and season with additional salt and pepper. Turn the lamb occasionally and cook to desired doneness, 5 to 6 minutes for medium-rare.

Divide the couscous among 4 plates. Remove the lamb from the grill and slide it off the skewers onto the couscous. Garnish with torn mint leaves.

# ROSEMARY-GRILLED VENISON WITH GRILLED PEACHES

SERVES 4 / In the past, venison has usually been considered a winter game meat, but the new farm-raised variety is lighter and works equally well in summer or spring.

1/4 CUP FINELY CRUSHED OR GROUND JUNIPER BERRIES (SEE SOURCES)

1/4 CUP FINELY CRUSHED OR GROUND STAR ANISE (SEE SOURCES)

1 VENISON LOIN, 1 1/2 TO 2 POUNDS (SEE SOURCES), CUT INTO 4 PORTIONS

KOSHER SALT

FRESHLY GROUND BLACK PEPPER

4 CUPS RUBY PORT

1/4 CUP VEAL DEMI-GLACE (SEE SOURCES), OR 1 CUP VEAL OR GAME STOCK

8 SPRIGS ROSEMARY

4 RIPE PEACHES, NECTARINES, PLUMS, OR APRICOTS, PITTED AND HALVED

EXTRA-VIRGIN OLIVE OIL FOR BRUSHING FRUIT

1 TABLESPOON BUTTER

In a small bowl, combine the crushed juniper berries and star anise. Season the venison with salt and pepper and coat with the juniper berry mixture, reserving 1 to 2 tablespoons for the sauce. Cover with plastic wrap, and refrigerate for about 1 hour.

In a medium saucepan over medium-high heat, bring the port to a boil. Decrease the heat and simmer until reduced to approximately 1/2 cup, 50 to 60 minutes. (Watch the port carefully near the end, as it contains sugar and burns quickly.) Pour the port into a small container and set aside. If you are using veal or game stock, rinse the saucepan, add the stock, and bring it to a boil over medium-high heat. Decrease the heat and simmer until it has reduced to 1/4 cup. (Or use 2 saucepans and reduce the port and the stock at the same time.) These reductions can be refrigerated for up to 2 days.

In a small saucepan, combine the demi-glace, 1 or 2 rosemary sprigs, and the reduced port, and season with salt and pepper. Add the reserved juniper berry and star anise mixture to taste. Keep the sauce warm over low heat.

Light a medium-hot fire in the grill.

Reserving a few for garnish, place the rosemary sprigs on the grill for a few seconds, just until they catch fire, and then remove, using tongs. Place the venison on the grill, and arrange the scorched rosemary sprigs on top. Grill the venison for about 5 minutes per side for medium-rare. Remove the meat from the grill and let it rest for 6 to 8 minutes before slicing. Discard the rosemary sprigs.

Meanwhile, brush the fruit halves with oil, season with salt and pepper, and place on the grill at the outer edges, where the heat is not as strong. Cook until the fruit is heated and tender throughout, 3 to 4 minutes per side.

Just before serving, remove the rosemary sprigs from the sauce. Swirl the butter into the sauce and taste for seasoning. Divide the sauce among 4 warmed plates. Cut the venison crosswise into thin slices and place over the sauce. Place 2 fruit halves on each plate, and garnish with the reserved rosemary sprigs.

# MAPLE-BALSAMIC
## GLAZED PORK CHOPS
### WITH PECANS AND GINGER

SERVES 4 / I wanted to create something totally American, yet suited to urban tastes and a little unexpected, in these pork chops. A simple but sophisticated glaze made with balsamic vinegar, maple syrup, brown sugar, and spices, brushed on the pork as it is grilling, turns out a caramelized, glistening chop. Candied pecans and ginger on top add texture, as do slices of grilled apple brushed with the same marinade.

1 CUP MAPLE SYRUP

1 TABLESPOON PLUS 1 TEASPOON
BALSAMIC VINEGAR

1 TABLESPOON PLUS 1 TEASPOON LIGHT
BROWN SUGAR

1/2 TEASPOON GROUND CINNAMON

1/2 CUP PECANS, TOASTED (PAGE 18)

4 PORK CHOPS, 1 INCH THICK
(PREFERABLY FROM NIMAN RANCH;
SEE SOURCES)

KOSHER SALT

FRESHLY GROUND BLACK PEPPER

EXTRA-VIRGIN OLIVE OIL FOR BRUSHING
PORK AND APPLES

2 GREEN APPLES

1/4 CUP FINELY DICED CANDIED GINGER
(SEE SOURCES)

POLENTA WITH GOAT CHEESE AND
ROSEMARY (PAGE 153; OPTIONAL)

Light a medium-hot fire in the grill. In a medium bowl, whisk together the maple syrup, balsamic vinegar, brown sugar, and cinnamon.

Place a small skillet over medium heat. Add the pecans and about 2 tablespoons of the maple mixture, stir gently to coat the nuts, and cook until the nuts are glazed, about 3 minutes. Remove the nuts to a plate and spread them out to cool. Chop very coarsely and set aside.

Season the pork chops with salt and pepper and brush with olive oil. Grill for 7 to 8 minutes per side for medium doneness. About 5 minutes before the chops are fully cooked, begin brushing them with the maple glaze and turning them (if you begin brushing them earlier, the glaze will burn).

While the chops are cooking, core the apples, but do not peel them. Slice them crosswise 1/2 inch thick. (Use an apple corer or slice the apple crosswise and then carefully cut out the core with a paring knife.) Lightly brush the apple slices with oil, season lightly with salt, and place on the grill. Brush with the maple glaze and grill for 2 to 3 minutes per side. They will soften and develop attractive grill marks.

When the chops are cooked, remove them from the grill and allow them to rest for 5 to 10 minutes before serving. Just before serving, brush the chops liberally with more maple glaze. Serve with the apple slices and sprinkle with the pecans and ginger. Accompany with Polenta with Goat Cheese and Rosemary, if desired.

# GRILLED
## FIGS WITH LEMON RICOTTA AND ROSEMARY SYRUP

SERVES 4 / In this unusual dish, the attractive grilled figs are slightly caramelized and glossy. Use the best ricotta you can find, preferably fresh rather than prepackaged. It will taste pure and sweet and will contrast beautifully with the grilled figs and herbal syrup.

1/2 CUP PLUS 2 TEASPOONS SUGAR

1/2 CUP WATER

1 TABLESPOON CHOPPED FRESH
    ROSEMARY

1 1/2 CUPS FRESH RICOTTA CHEESE

2 TEASPOONS GRATED LEMON ZEST

PINCH OF SALT

8 LARGE RIPE FIGS, ABOUT 1 POUND
    TOTAL, STEMMED AND HALVED

EXTRA-VIRGIN OLIVE OIL FOR BRUSHING
    GRILL AND FIGS

In a medium saucepan over high heat, combine 1/2 cup of the sugar with the water and bring to a boil, stirring until the sugar is dissolved. Add the chopped rosemary, decrease the heat to medium-low, and simmer for 10 minutes. Allow the syrup to cool, then strain through a fine sieve to remove the rosemary. The syrup can be refrigerated, covered, for up to 1 week.

Light a medium-hot fire in the grill.

In a medium bowl, combine the ricotta, lemon zest, the remaining 2 teaspoons sugar, and salt. Set aside.

Brush the grill and the figs with oil, and place the figs cut-side down on the grill. After a minute or so, start checking the figs to look for nicely browned grill marks. (This may happen quickly or it may take longer, depending on the heat of your grill.) Don't worry if the figs char slightly—it enhances their flavor. When the cut-sides have browned, carefully flip the figs and cook until soft, 1 to 2 minutes more.

To serve, divide the ricotta mixture among 4 serving plates. Arrange the figs cut-side up around the ricotta and drizzle the rosemary syrup over all. The figs are best when served warm.

# BITTERSWEET CHOCOLATE BRUSCHETTA

**SERVES 4 /** Bread and chocolate are two of my favorite foods, and I love combining them into this sweet, crunchy dessert or snack. This is a very flexible recipe—see the variations for fruit and nut suggestions.

4 SLICES RUSTIC-STYLE WHITE BREAD, 3/4 INCH THICK

3 TABLESPOONS BUTTER, MELTED, OR SUBSTITUTE ALMOND, HAZELNUT, OR OTHER NUT OIL

KOSHER SALT

7 OUNCES GOOD-QUALITY BITTERSWEET CHOCOLATE, SUCH AS CALLEBAUT (SEE SOURCES), ROUGHLY CHOPPED

1 PINT STRAWBERRIES, HULLED AND THINLY SLICED

1/4 CUP HAZELNUTS, TOASTED (PAGE 18) AND COARSELY CHOPPED

Light a medium-hot fire in the grill.

Brush both sides of the bread with the melted butter, and sprinkle lightly with salt. Grill on one side until toasted, with golden brown grill marks. Flip the bread and top each slice with chopped chocolate. Grill until the chocolate is melted and the bread is toasted on the bottom. Cover the grill briefly, if desired, to melt the chocolate more quickly. Remove the bread from the grill, top with sliced strawberries, and sprinkle with chopped hazelnuts.

### VARIATIONS

Substitute an equal amount of raspberries or 2 bananas for the strawberries. Substitute chopped walnuts or almonds for the hazelnuts.

Substitute milk chocolate or Gianduja (see Sources) for the bittersweet chocolate.

CHAPTER 5/
ROASTING FAST AND SLOW

# ROASTING FAST AND SLOW

Myth has it that rich and fragrant roasts, casseroles, and baked desserts are best produced in a rambling farmhouse kitchen. But we know the truth: Home is where you light the oven, whatever its size.

Roasting is a completely different technique from sautéing and grilling, where food comes into direct contact with heat and is caramelized or browned. Here we are trying to envelop our dish with heat so that it cooks uniformly and the flavors meld.

It is important to understand whether the roasting process will be fast or slow, and why. Parmigiano-Reggiano Pudding (page 112), for example, is a custard that has to be brought along slowly so it that won't curdle or overcook. Chocolate Ganache Cake (page 128), Banana Cake (page 130), and Amaretto Milk-Soaked Cake (page 131) require care, and Truffled Macaroni and Cheese (page 116), while somewhat heartier, also needs slow cooking. But with pizza, meats, and some fish, you get a chance to be a little more forceful.

Seasoning is critical in oven-cooked dishes, because there's not a lot of chance to make up for your errors at the end. Nor do you have as much of an opportunity to rearrange proportions of ingredients after the food is cooked. The good part is that once you put these dishes into the oven, they don't require a lot of fuss.

For a lot of people, home cooking means roasting a chicken, throwing together a meatloaf, or whipping up a casserole of macaroni and cheese. The next time you want to make one of these classics, try my versions or branch out with the unusual Warm Goat Cheese Tarts with Fig Jam and Rosemary (page 110); Roasted Lamb Loin Stuffed with Almonds, Dates, Goat Cheese, and Mint (page 124); and Coriander-Crusted Pork Loin Stuffed with Dried Peaches and Pine Nuts (page 126). And here are two exciting ways to roast a familiar fish: Salt-Baked Salmon (page 121) and Slow-Roasted Salmon with Yogurt and Cardamom (page 120).

# WARM GOAT CHEESE TARTS
## WITH FIG JAM AND ROSEMARY

SERVES 4 / This savory and sweet appetizer has great textural contrast, with the crisp pastry and the soft, warm goat cheese. The combination of fruit and cheese makes a satisfying light lunch, perhaps with a fresh green salad, or an elegant first course.

### FIG JAM

1 TABLESPOON EXTRA-VIRGIN OLIVE OIL
1/2 MEDIUM SHALLOT, FINELY CHOPPED
3/4 POUND FRESH FIGS (5 TO 7 FIGS), DICED
1/3 CUP RUBY PORT
2 TABLESPOONS AGED BALSAMIC VINEGAR (TRY LULU FIG BALSAMIC VINEGAR, SEE SOURCES), PLUS EXTRA FOR DRIZZLING OVER TARTS
KOSHER SALT
FRESHLY GROUND BLACK PEPPER

### TARTS

1 SHEET PURCHASED PUFF PASTRY (8 TO 9 OUNCES), THAWED
1 EGG YOLK
1 TABLESPOON WATER
KOSHER SALT
4 OUNCES SOFT GOAT CHEESE
1 TEASPOON MINCED FRESH ROSEMARY
FRESHLY GROUND BLACK PEPPER
2 FIGS, THINLY SLICED

### TO MAKE THE JAM

Heat the olive oil in a medium skillet over medium-high heat and cook the shallot, stirring occasionally, until translucent, 1 to 2 minutes. Add the diced figs and cook, stirring occasionally, 2 to 3 minutes. Add the port, bring to a boil, and reduce the heat to medium-low. Simmer until the port has reduced to a syrupy consistency and the figs have broken down, about 10 minutes. Remove from the heat, stir in 2 tablespoons balsamic vinegar, season with salt and pepper, and set aside to cool. You should have about 1 cup—more than you need; save the remainder for another use. It can be refrigerated in an airtight container for up to 1 week.

### TO MAKE THE TARTS

Preheat the oven to 400°F. Place the puff pastry sheet on a lightly floured surface. Cut out 4 rounds, using a 4-inch round cutter; a clean, dry empty can; or a sharp knife. Lightly flour a rolling pin and roll each piece of pastry out to about 6 inches in diameter. (The tarts will shrink while baking.)

Carefully transfer the pastry rounds to an ungreased baking sheet and pierce them all over with a fork.

In a small bowl, beat the egg yolk with the water. Brush the tops of the pastry rounds with the egg wash, sprinkle lightly with salt, and bake until golden brown, about 12 minutes. Remove from the oven and set aside to cool.

In a small bowl, mix the goat cheese with the rosemary and season well with salt and pepper.

Preheat the broiler.

Spread the fig jam over the pastry rounds, leaving only a very narrow border, and crumble the goat cheese mixture over the top. Place the tarts back on the baking sheet and broil until they are heated and the goat cheese is nicely browned, 1 to 2 minutes.

### TO SERVE

Place a tart on each of 4 plates, top with the fig slices, and drizzle with balsamic vinegar.

# PARMIGIANO-REGGIANO PUDDING

**SERVES 4 /** Any way you serve this velvety custard, it brings richness and elegance to the table. Try it as a first course with lightly dressed baby spinach leaves or steamed asparagus, or as an ethereal garnish for rack of lamb or roast chicken. You need only a little bit to accessorize a simple dish—like a beautiful piece of fine jewelry.

2 EGG YOLKS PLUS 1 EGG

3/4 CUP HEAVY CREAM

1 TABLESPOON BUTTER

2 TABLESPOONS FLOUR

1/4 CUP MILK

3/4 CUP LIGHT CREAM

2/3 CUP FINELY GRATED PARMIGIANO-
REGGIANO CHEESE

1/4 TEASPOON KOSHER SALT

1/8 TEASPOON FRESHLY GROUND WHITE
PEPPER

Preheat the oven to 225°F. Bring a large pot of water to a boil over high heat. Butter four 6-ounce ramekins.

In a medium bowl, whisk the egg yolks and the whole egg with the heavy cream and set aside.

In a medium saucepan, melt the butter over medium heat. Whisk in the flour and cook, stirring, for 3 minutes. Remove from the heat and slowly whisk in the milk and light cream; then whisk in the egg yolk and heavy cream mixture.

Add the Parmigiano-Reggiano, stirring until fully incorporated. Stir in the salt and pepper and pour the mixture into the ramekins. Place the ramekins in a large pan and fill the pan with enough boiling water to come two-thirds up their sides. Cover with foil and bake until somewhat firm and a knife inserted in the center comes out clean, about 1 hour and 15 minutes. Serve the custards in the ramekins.

# BLT PIZZA

SERVES 4 AS A FIRST COURSE, 2 AS A MAIN COURSE / Bacon, lettuce, and tomatoes are great together in sandwiches; why not serve them on a crisp pizza crust? This recipe uses the classic combination of ingredients, with the addition of a little mozzarella, and with arugula standing in for the traditional lettuce. | The cornmeal is not absolutely necessary, but it helps the finished pizza slide easily off the pan or stone, and it adds a little extra flavor and texture to the crust.

3 SLICES BACON, PREFERABLY NIMAN RANCH (SEE SOURCES)

1/4 RECIPE PIZZA DOUGH (PAGE 114)

2 TABLESPOONS CORNMEAL

1 TEASPOON EXTRA-VIRGIN OLIVE OIL, PLUS ADDITIONAL FOR BRUSHING DOUGH

1 LARGE VINE-RIPENED TOMATO, THINLY SLICED (USE AN HEIRLOOM TOMATO, IF AVAILABLE)

KOSHER SALT

1/2 CUP SHREDDED FRESH BUFFALO MOZZARELLA, OR SUBSTITUTE REGULAR MOZZARELLA

1/2 BUNCH ARUGULA

1/8 TEASPOON DRIED HOT RED PEPPER FLAKES

FRESHLY GROUND BLACK PEPPER

Preheat the oven to 550°F, or as high as your oven will allow. Set out a pizza stone, or oil a baking sheet.

Heat a medium skillet over medium-high heat and cook the bacon slices on both sides until crisp. Drain on paper towels and set aside.

Roll out the dough on a lightly floured surface to a round shape with a diameter of about 10 inches. Sprinkle the cornmeal over the pizza stone or oiled baking sheet, covering approximately the area the pizza dough will cover. Place the dough over the cornmeal and lightly brush the surface of the dough with olive oil.

Arrange the tomato slices over the dough and season lightly with salt. Spread the cheese over the tomatoes. Break the bacon slices into small pieces and sprinkle over the cheese. In a small bowl, toss the arugula with 1 teaspoon of olive oil and sprinkle lightly with salt. Arrange the arugula over the pizza and bake until the crust is nicely browned, 8 to 10 minutes. Remove from the oven, sprinkle with pepper flakes, season with pepper, and serve immediately.

# WILD MUSHROOM PIZZA

MAKES ENOUGH DOUGH FOR 4 PIZZAS (SAVE THE REST), ENOUGH TOPPING FOR 1 PIZZA. EACH PIZZA SERVES 4 AS A FIRST COURSE, 2 AS A MAIN COURSE / In Maine, where I grew up, pizza always meant garlicky tomato sauce and strings of hot, melted cheese. But when I tasted pizza in Italy, and discovered Wolfgang Puck's pizzas in California, I realized that a base of crisp, baked dough can be a great carrier for all sorts of other flavors. The best earthy wild mushrooms and sharp Asiago cheese, preferably from Wisconsin, make this version delicious and satisfying. | This pizza is not heavily dressed—it isn't completely covered with mushrooms and suffocated by a blanket of cheese. Rather, there is a surprise in each bite: you may get a taste of cheese or mushrooms, a bite of crisp crust, or a little truffle oil.

## PIZZA DOUGH

1¹/₂ CUPS LUKEWARM WATER

¹/₂ TEASPOON DRY YEAST

APPROXIMATELY 4 CUPS FLOUR

¹/₄ TEASPOON SALT

2 TABLESPOONS OLIVE OIL

## TOPPING

2 TABLESPOONS EXTRA-VIRGIN OLIVE
   OIL, PLUS ADDITIONAL FOR BRUSHING
   DOUGH

¹/₂ POUND MIXED WILD MUSHROOMS,
   SUCH AS SHIITAKE, CHANTERELLES,
   OR OYSTER, STEMS TRIMMED AND
   CAPS CUT INTO THICK SLICES IF LARGE

KOSHER SALT

FRESHLY GROUND BLACK PEPPER

2 TABLESPOONS CORNMEAL

1 CUP SHREDDED ASIAGO CHEESE
   (4 OUNCES)

¹/₈ TEASPOON DRIED HOT RED PEPPER
   FLAKES

¹/₄ CUP COARSELY CHOPPED FLAT-LEAF
   PARSLEY

1 TABLESPOON TRUFFLE OIL (SEE
   SOURCES; OPTIONAL)

## TO MAKE THE DOUGH

Place the water in a large bowl and stir in the yeast with a wooden spoon until dissolved. Add 1 cup of the flour, stirring constantly in one direction until incorporated. Stir in another cup of flour, then stir 100 times in the same direction, about 2 minutes. This will help develop the gluten. Cover the dough with plastic wrap and let stand at room temperature for at least 30 minutes or up to 3 hours.

Sprinkle the salt and oil over the dough and add more flour, stirring in about ¹/₂ cup at a time until incorporated. When the dough is heavy and too hard to stir, turn it onto a floured board and knead, adding extra flour as necessary to prevent sticking, for 10 minutes, or until smooth.

Put the dough in a large bowl, cover with plastic wrap, and let it rise until more than doubled in volume, at least 3 hours. Cut the dough into quarters. (Can be refrigerated, wrapped tightly in plastic, for up to 2 days or frozen for up to 1 month.)

## TO MAKE THE PIZZA

Preheat the oven to 550°F or as high as your oven will allow. Set out a pizza stone, or oil a baking sheet.

Heat 2 tablespoons of the olive oil in a large skillet over medium-high heat and sauté the mushrooms until softened and beginning to brown, 4 to 5 minutes. Remove from the heat, season with salt and pepper, and set aside. Roll out one-fourth of the dough on a lightly floured surface to a round shape with a diameter of about 10 inches. Sprinkle the cornmeal over the pizza stone or oiled baking sheet, covering approximately the area the pizza dough will cover. Place the dough over the cornmeal and brush the surface lightly with olive oil. Sprinkle with half of the cheese.

Top with the mushrooms and the remaining cheese. Bake until the crust is nicely browned, 8 to 10 minutes.

Remove the pizza from the oven and sprinkle with the red pepper flakes and chopped parsley. Drizzle with the truffle oil, if desired, and serve immediately.

# TRUFFLED MACARONI AND CHEESE

SERVES 8 TO 10 AS A SIDE DISH, 4 TO 6 AS A MAIN COURSE / This has been one of the most popular dishes at Commune in New York. As a side dish, it makes an elegant accompaniment to simple roast chicken, lamb, or beef, but it is also great all by itself. It is convenient to serve at home, since it can be mixed ahead, refrigerated, and then cooked when you need it. Be sure to use a ribbed pasta, so the sauce will adhere.

1 POUND GARGANELLI PASTA (SEE SOURCES), OR SUBSTITUTE PENNE RIGATE

7 TABLESPOONS BUTTER

6 TABLESPOONS FLOUR

3 3/4 CUPS WHOLE MILK

KOSHER SALT

FRESHLY GROUND BLACK PEPPER

1/2 TEASPOON GRATED NUTMEG

1 1/2 CUPS GRATED ASIAGO CHEESE

1/4 CUP TRUFFLE BUTTER (SEE SOURCES)

1/2 CUP FRESH BREAD CRUMBS

WHITE TRUFFLE OIL (OPTIONAL; SEE SOURCES)

Preheat the oven to 400°F. Lightly butter 6 individual ramekins, or substitute a 9-by-13-inch baking dish.

Bring a large pot of salted water to a boil and cook the pasta until al dente, 5 to 6 minutes (or about 80 percent of the time given in the package directions). Drain and spread the pasta out on a baking sheet or tray to cool it and stop the cooking.

In a medium saucepan, melt 5 tablespoons of the butter over medium heat. Whisk in the flour and cook, stirring, for 3 minutes. Whisk in the milk and increase the heat to high. When the milk begins to boil, decrease the heat to low and continue to cook, stirring, until thickened, 1 to 2 minutes. Season with salt, pepper, and grated nutmeg.

In a large mixing bowl, combine the cooked pasta, Asiago, truffle butter, and sauce. Taste and reseason, if desired.

Spoon the pasta mixture into the prepared ramekins or baking dish, top with the bread crumbs, and dot lightly with the remaining 2 tablespoons butter. Bake until hot and lightly browned, 35 to 40 minutes.

Drizzle the baked pasta with white truffle oil, if desired, and serve.

# BAKED PASTA
## WITH ZUCCHINI AND ASIAGO

SERVES 4 TO 6 AS A MAIN COURSE, 8 TO 10 AS A SIDE DISH / This summery dish is a slightly more refined version of the macaroni and cheese that I grew up with. It's ideal for home entertaining because you can put it together, refrigerate it, and then pop it in the oven when you're ready to serve. Or you can bake it ahead and reheat it or even eat it cold as a lunch—this is not a delicate dish.

1 POUND GEMELLI PASTA (SEE SOURCES), OR SUBSTITUTE FUSILLI OR CAVATELLI

2 MEDIUM ZUCCHINI, ABOUT 1 POUND TOTAL

2 TABLESPOONS EXTRA-VIRGIN OLIVE OIL

KOSHER SALT

FRESHLY GROUND BLACK PEPPER

3 TABLESPOONS BUTTER

3 TABLESPOONS FLOUR

2 CUPS WHOLE MILK

$^1/_4$ TEASPOON GRATED NUTMEG

2 CUPS GRATED AGED ASIAGO CHEESE

$^1/_4$ CUP SUN-DRIED TOMATOES PACKED IN OLIVE OIL, DRAINED AND ROUGHLY CHOPPED

$^1/_2$ CUP FRESH SOURDOUGH BREAD CRUMBS (FROM ABOUT 2 SLICES)

2 TABLESPOONS COARSELY CHOPPED FLAT-LEAF PARSLEY

Preheat the oven to 400°F. Lightly butter a 9-by-13-inch baking dish.

Bring a large pot of salted water to a boil and cook the pasta until al dente, 5 to 6 minutes (or 80 percent of the time given on the package). Drain and spread the pasta out on a baking sheet or tray to cool it and stop the cooking process.

Holding the zucchini upright, slice the outer flesh down from top to bottom along one side, without cutting into the core. Rotate the zucchini slightly and slice again, cutting 4 top-to-bottom slices in all. The outer side of each long slice will be curved; the inner side will be flat. Cut each slice crosswise into $^1/_8$-inch, half-moon-shaped slices.

In a sauté pan, heat the olive oil over medium-high heat and sauté the zucchini until lightly translucent, about 3 minutes. Season with salt and pepper.

In a medium saucepan, melt the butter over medium heat. Whisk in the flour and cook, stirring, for 1 to 2 minutes. Whisk in the milk and increase the heat to high. When the milk begins to boil, decrease the heat to low and continue to cook, stirring, until thickened, 1 to 2 minutes. Season with salt, pepper, and grated nutmeg. In a large mixing bowl, combine the cooked pasta, cheese, tomatoes, zucchini, and sauce. Taste and reseason, if desired.

Spoon the pasta mixture into the prepared baking dish, top with the bread crumbs, and bake until hot and lightly browned, 35 to 40 minutes.

Garnish with chopped parsley and serve.

# HALIBUT BAKED IN PARCHMENT

## WITH TOMATOES, LIME, AND CILANTRO

SERVES 4 / With very few ingredients and straightforward fresh flavors, this is a delicate dish. It is easily put together and the packets can be made a little in advance (though not too far ahead, because the tomatoes will release liquid as they wait). | The method is a variation of the French classic method of cooking *en papillote,* in which food is wrapped and cooked in parchment paper. You can substitute aluminum foil if necessary. | The tomatoes for this dish have to be great—beautiful and perfectly ripe.

EXTRA-VIRGIN OLIVE OIL FOR BRUSHING BAKING SHEETS AND DRIZZLING OVER FISH

3 LIMES

4 HALIBUT FILLETS, 6 TO 7 OUNCES EACH, OR SUBSTITUTE HALIBUT STEAKS, CENTER BONE CUT OUT AND SKIN REMOVED (YOUR FISHMONGER CAN DO THIS) OR CHILEAN SEA BASS FILLETS

KOSHER SALT

FRESHLY GROUND BLACK PEPPER

2 MEDIUM VINE-RIPENED TOMATOES OR 4 PLUM TOMATOES, SEEDED AND CUT INTO LARGE DICE, OR SUBSTITUTE GOLDEN OR HEIRLOOM TOMATOES

1/4 CUP WHITE WINE

1 EGG WHITE, LIGHTLY BEATEN

1/2 CUP LOOSELY PACKED CILANTRO LEAVES, OR SUBSTITUTE BASIL

Preheat the oven to 400°F if cooking immediately.

Lightly brush 2 baking sheets with olive or canola oil. Cut 4 circles of parchment paper about 14 inches in diameter.

Segment 2 of the limes: Cut the peel from the top and bottom and stand each lime upright on a cutting board. With a small, sharp paring knife, gently slice away the peel down to the flesh. Cut along each side of the membranes to separate the segments. Cut each segment into 2 or 3 pieces and set aside.

Juice the third lime and set the juice aside.

Season the fish with salt and pepper. Lightly brush one half of each parchment circle with extra-virgin olive oil, covering an area large enough to hold a fillet. Place a fillet on the oiled side of each parchment circle. Divide the tomatoes and lime segments over the top of the fillets, and pour a splash of white wine over each.

Lightly brush the edges of the parchment circles with egg white. Fold the parchment over the fish and seal the edges by making a series of 1- or 2-inch folds, each sealing the one before. The packages should be tightly sealed, yet there should be plenty of room around the fish. (At this point the packages can be refrigerated for up to 2 hours. Preheat the oven to 400°F before proceeding.)

Place 2 packages on each baking sheet, lightly brush the packages with oil, and bake in the oven for 15 minutes. The packages should puff and brown slightly.

To serve, carefully cut each package open and gently transfer the contents to a warmed plate. There will be a lot of flavorful liquid and you may want to spoon some of it over the fish. Top each fillet with a splash of lime juice and drizzle extra-virgin olive oil over and around it. Sprinkle with cilantro and serve.

# SLOW-ROASTED SALMON WITH YOGURT AND CARDAMOM

**SERVES 4 /** First bathed in yogurt and then slowly roasted, salmon becomes creamy, delicate, and rich. This is a sensual main course, spicy without being hot, and it is my favorite way of cooking salmon at home.

4 SALMON FILLETS, 6 TO 7 OUNCES
   EACH, SKIN REMOVED (YOUR FISH-
   MONGER CAN DO THIS)
2 TABLESPOONS EXTRA-VIRGIN OLIVE
   OIL, PLUS ADDITIONAL FOR BRUSHING
   FILLETS
2 TEASPOONS GROUND CARDAMOM
1 CUP PLAIN YOGURT
2 TABLESPOONS HONEY
KOSHER SALT
COARSELY GROUND BLACK PEPPER

Brush the top of each fillet with olive oil and sprinkle evenly with the cardamom. Place the fillets side by side in a large glass baking dish or a platter.

In a small bowl, mix the yogurt and honey and spoon liberally over the top of each fillet. Wrap the baking dish tightly in plastic wrap and refrigerate for at least 3 hours and up to 6 hours (any longer and the yogurt will begin to break down the fish).

Preheat the oven to 325°F.

Unwrap the salmon and brush off the excess yogurt. Season with salt and pepper.

Heat the 2 tablespoons olive oil over medium-high heat in a large skillet (preferably nonstick, with an ovenproof handle) and sear the salmon on one side until it begins to caramelize, 2 to 3 minutes (use 2 pans, if necessary, to avoid crowding the fillets). Flip the salmon over and place the pan in the oven for about 6 minutes, or until the salmon is pink, translucent, and lightly cooked through; or for approximately 8 minutes, until it is entirely cooked through, depending on desired doneness. Place each fillet on a warmed plate.

# SALT-BAKED SALMON

SERVES 6 / I first tasted salt-baked fish in Turkey and Greece and admired its rich, intense flavor and moist texture. It is slightly salty, which I love because the brininess makes me feel close to the ocean. The fish doesn't need any sauce; just brush off the salt crust and it is ready to serve.

1 LARGE SALMON FILLET, 2 TO 3 POUNDS,
   SKIN REMOVED (THE FISHMONGER
   CAN DO THIS)
FRESHLY GROUND BLACK PEPPER
3 CUPS KOSHER SALT OR COARSE SEA
   SALT

Preheat the oven to 450°F. Season the salmon with pepper.

Pour 1 1/2 cups of the salt into a glass baking dish or onto a baking sheet in an even layer about 1/4 inch thick and just slightly larger than the salmon. Lay the fillet on the salt and pour the remaining salt over it to cover completely.

Bake the salmon for 15 to 20 minutes for rare to medium, or about 25 minutes for medium-well. Brush off all the salt, and divide the salmon among 6 warmed plates.

# CHEDDAR MEATLOAF

SERVES 4 / We all know the magic that Cheddar works on hamburger, and this dish elevates the concept. The light, herbaceous, perfectly spiced loaf is rolled around a savory Cheddar stuffing and accented with the deep tomato flavor of your favorite homemade tomato sauce. | Be sure to use the freshest ground beef, fresh rosemary, and a really good Cheddar, such as Grafton or Montgomery (see Sources).

1 POUND GROUND BEEF

1 CUP DRY BREAD CRUMBS

1/2 CUP FINELY CHOPPED ONION

2 TEASPOONS FINELY CHOPPED GARLIC

1/3 CUP KETCHUP

1 TABLESPOON WORCESTERSHIRE SAUCE

1 TEASPOON TABASCO SAUCE

1 EGG, LIGHLY BEATEN

1 TEASPOON FINELY CHOPPED ROSEMARY

2 TEASPOONS KOSHER SALT

1/2 TEASPOON FRESHLY GROUND BLACK PEPPER

1 1/3 CUPS COARSELY SHREDDED CHEDDAR CHEESE (ABOUT 1/3 POUND)

1 CUP CHUNKY TOMATO SAUCE (PAGE 155), WARMED, OR GOOD-QUALITY PURCHASED SAUCE

Preheat the oven to 400°F. In a large mixing bowl, combine the beef, bread crumbs, onion, garlic, ketchup, Worcestershire, Tabasco, egg, rosemary, salt, and pepper. On a sheet of parchment or waxed paper, pat out the meat into a rectangle approximately 9 by 12 inches. Sprinkle the cheese over the meat, leaving a thin border all around. Roll tightly, as for a jelly roll, keeping your hand under the parchment to guide the roll, and pinch the edges together to seal. (Even if the roll does not close tightly, keep the seam on top. The melting cheese is very attractive). Carefully transfer to a loaf pan and bake until a meat thermometer inserted in the center reads 140°F, about 45 minutes.

To serve, slice the meatloaf and spoon tomato sauce over each portion.

# ROAST CHICKEN WITH LEMON, SAGE, AND PINE NUTS

**SERVES 4** / Simple and elegant describe the city cook's repertoire, but a bit of innovation is important, too. We took some incredible organic chicken and decided to dress it up with a pesto-like stuffing of lemon, sage, and pine nuts under the skin. The chicken is equally delicious served cold the next day.

1/2 CUP PINE NUTS, TOASTED (PAGE 18)

2 TABLESPOONS GRATED LEMON ZEST

2 1/2 TABLESPOONS CHOPPED FRESH SAGE

2 TABLESPOONS BUTTER, AT ROOM TEMPERATURE

KOSHER SALT

FRESHLY GROUND BLACK PEPPER

1 CHICKEN, 3 POUNDS, RINSED AND PATTED DRY

2 TABLESPOONS EXTRA-VIRGIN OLIVE OIL

Preheat the oven to 450°F.

Put the toasted pine nuts, lemon zest, and sage in the bowl of a food processor (a miniprocessor works best for these small quantities), and process until finely chopped. Add the butter and process to combine. Season with salt and pepper and process again briefly. (You can also use a mortar and pestle, or chop the ingredients finely by hand and combine them well in a bowl, using a wooden spoon.)

Season the inside of the chicken with salt and pepper. Starting at the neck end, slide your fingers under the skin of the breast and upper part of the legs and spread the butter mixture under the skin to cover the meat. Tie the ends of the legs together with kitchen string.

Heat the olive oil in a large skillet (with an ovenproof handle) or roasting pan over medium-high heat. Season the outside of the chicken with salt and pepper. When the oil is hot, brown the chicken on one side, about 5 minutes. Check to make sure the skin is not burning. Flip the chicken to brown the other side, again cooking for 5 minutes. Turn the chicken on its back, put it in the oven, and roast until the chicken is golden brown and the juices run clear, 35 to 45 minutes. Remove from the oven and let rest for 5 to 10 minutes before carving.

# ROASTED LAMB LOIN
## STUFFED WITH ALMONDS, DATES, GOAT CHEESE, AND MINT

SERVES 4 / These thin lamb loins with their flavorful stuffing cook quickly, and the finished dish is colorful and delicious. It is rustic rather than fancy, drizzled with a simple orange and honey vinaigrette and garnished with chewy chopped dates and toasted almonds. | The meat and stuffing are tied together, not rolled, so slice carefully. But don't worry if the package falls apart a little—it will still be beautiful, especially when arranged on a large serving platter. | This goes well with farro (page 143) or Couscous with Toasted Almonds and Cumin (page 162).

### LAMB

2 LAMB LOINS, ABOUT 10 OUNCES EACH, TRIMMED, LEAVING A THIN LAYER OF FAT (SEE SOURCES)

KOSHER SALT

FRESHLY GROUND BLACK PEPPER

2 OUNCES SOFT GOAT CHEESE

1 1/2 TABLESPOONS COARSELY CHOPPED OR TORN MINT LEAVES

3/4 CUP ALMONDS, TOASTED (PAGE 18)

1/2 CUP COARSELY CHOPPED PITTED DATES

2 TABLESPOONS EXTRA-VIRGIN OLIVE OIL

### VINAIGRETTE

1/2 CUP FRESHLY SQUEEZED ORANGE JUICE

2 TABLESPOONS HONEY

1/4 CUP LOOSELY PACKED CILANTRO LEAVES

2 TABLESPOONS EXTRA-VIRGIN OLIVE OIL

### TO ROAST THE LAMB

Preheat the oven to 400°F.

Place each lamb loin between 2 sheets of plastic wrap and, using a meat mallet, pound to a thickness of about 3/4 inch (or pound with the bottom of a bottle, but use caution). Lay one of the pounded lamb loins flat on a work surface. Season with salt and pepper and spread with the goat cheese, leaving a 1/2-inch border all around. Top with the mint and about half of the chopped almonds and dates, reserving the rest for garnish. Season the other loin with salt and pepper and place seasoned-side down on top of the first loin, overlapping the edges as much as possible so the filling will not come out. Tie crosswise tightly with kitchen twine at about 3/4-inch intervals, and season all over with salt and pepper.

Heat 2 tablespoons of the olive oil in a large skillet (with an ovenproof handle) over medium-high heat. When the oil is hot, sear the lamb loin for 1 to 2 minutes per side. Place the skillet in the oven and roast for 12 to 15 minutes. Remove from the oven and allow to rest for 5 to 7 minutes.

### TO MAKE THE VINAIGRETTE

Combine the orange juice, honey, and cilantro leaves in a medium nonreactive bowl. Whisk in the remaining 2 tablespoons of olive oil in a steady stream, and season with salt and pepper. Keep the vinaigrette at room temperature before serving, so it won't cool down the lamb.

### TO SERVE

Remove the string and cut the lamb into 3/4-inch slices, carefully cutting straight up and down. Arrange the slices on a large platter or on 4 serving plates and drizzle the vinaigrette generously around them (the meat will soak up a lot of vinaigrette). Sprinkle with the remaining chopped dates and toasted almonds.

# CORIANDER-CRUSTED PORK LOIN

## STUFFED WITH DRIED PEACHES AND PINE NUTS

**SERVES 6** / This dish is a variation of a popular recipe in my first book. Here I use peaches and pine nuts in place of the earlier combination of apricots and pistachios, and coat the meat with coriander instead of cumin. This version goes especially well with Polenta with Goat Cheese and Rosemary. | Be careful not to overcook—the days of dried-out pork are past. Trimming most of the fat allows the pork to cook more quickly, and the meat will be juicy and tender.

10 DRIED PEACH HALVES, OR SUBSTITUTE
   DRIED NECTARINE HALVES OR 1 CUP
   DRIED APRICOTS

1/3 CUP PINE NUTS, TOASTED (PAGE 18),
   OR SUBSTITUTE WALNUTS

KOSHER SALT

FRESHLY GROUND BLACK PEPPER

1 BONELESS PORK LOIN (ABOUT
   3 POUNDS), WELL TRIMMED, WITH
   JUST A THIN LAYER OF FAT LEFT
   ON THE OUTSIDE

2 TABLESPOONS FINELY CHOPPED
   PEELED FRESH GINGER, PLUS
   1 TABLESPOON COARSELY CHOPPED
   OR SLICED PEELED FRESH GINGER

1 TABLESPOON FINELY CHOPPED
   ROSEMARY

5 TABLESPOONS EXTRA-VIRGIN OLIVE
   OIL

2 TABLESPOONS CORIANDER SEEDS,
   COARSELY CRACKED (WRAP THEM
   IN A DISH TOWEL AND SMASH WITH
   A HEAVY PAN)

1 RIB CELERY, COARSELY CHOPPED

1 MEDIUM CARROT, PEELED AND
   COARSELY CHOPPED

Bring 3 cups of water to boil in a small saucepan and add the dried peaches. Remove the pan from the heat, allow the peaches to soften for about 10 minutes, and drain. Cut 6 of the peach halves into half-inch dice (reserve the remaining peach halves for the sauce). Put the diced peaches into a small bowl and add the pine nuts, 1/2 teaspoon salt, and 1/4 teaspoon pepper.

Butterfly the pork by making a lengthwise incision from the top of the loin all the way through the meat to within 1/2 inch of the bottom. Spread open the cut meat. In a small bowl, mix the finely chopped ginger, the rosemary, 2 tablespoons of the olive oil, 1/2 teaspoon salt, and 1/4 teaspoon pepper. Rub the inside of the pork with the ginger-rosemary mixture.

Spread the peach–pine nut mixture evenly inside the loin. Close up the meat and tie it tightly with kitchen string both crosswise and lengthwise. Season the loin with salt and pepper. Spread the cracked coriander seeds on a cutting board or platter and roll the loin in the seeds.

Preheat the oven to 500°F.

In a large skillet (with an ovenproof handle) over medium-high heat, heat 2 tablespoons of the olive oil and brown the pork loin on all sides, 6 to 8 minutes total. Place the skillet in the oven and roast the meat to a temperature of 135° to 140°F, 20 to 25 minutes. It will be cooked through and slightly pink in the center around the stuffing (although you should not slice it yet). Cover the meat with foil and let it rest at room temperature for about 15 minutes; it will continue to cook as it sits.

1/2 CUP WHITE WINE

1 1/2 CUPS CHICKEN STOCK OR CANNED
   LOW-SODIUM BROTH

1 TABLESPOON FRESHLY SQUEEZED
   LEMON JUICE

1 TABLESPOON BUTTER (OPTIONAL)

POLENTA WITH GOAT CHEESE AND
   ROSEMARY (PAGE 153) AS ACCOM-
   PANIMENT

Meanwhile, heat the remaining tablespoon of olive oil in a medium skillet over medium-high heat and add the celery, carrot, coarsely chopped ginger, and reserved peach halves. Sauté for 3 to 5 minutes. Add the wine and cook until most of the liquid has evaporated, scraping up any browned bits from the bottom of the pan, about 5 minutes. Add the chicken stock and lemon juice, bring to a boil, and cook until reduced to about 3/4 cup, 8 to 10 minutes. Remove the peach halves from the sauce and cut into half-inch dice. Strain the sauce into a medium bowl, discarding the remaining solids.

Return the sauce to the pan, add the diced peach halves, and season with salt and pepper. Stir in the butter for extra richness and flavor, if desired.

Cut the pork crosswise into half-inch slices and place 2 slices on each of 6 plates. Spoon the sauce over the pork. Serve with the polenta.

# CHOCOLATE GANACHE CAKE
## WITH WHIPPED CREAM

SERVES 12 / Very rich, chocolatey, and dense, this cake is a perfect party dessert or a special treat. The chocolate and almond flavors work beautifully together and shine through, no matter what temperature the cake is served at.

### CAKE

1/2 POUND (2 STICKS) BUTTER, CUT INTO PIECES, PLUS MORE FOR PAN

8 OUNCES GOOD-QUALITY BITTERSWEET OR SEMISWEET CHOCOLATE, SUCH AS CALLEBAUT (SEE SOURCES), COARSELY CHOPPED

4 EGGS, SEPARATED

2/3 CUP SUGAR

1/4 CUP TOASTED ALMOND FLOUR (SEE NOTE AND SOURCES)

1/2 TEASPOON GROUND CINNAMON

1/4 TEASPOON SALT

POWDERED SUGAR FOR DUSTING (OPTIONAL)

### WHIPPED CREAM

1 1/2 CUPS HEAVY CREAM, CHILLED

2 TABLESPOONS POWDERED SUGAR

1 TEASPOON PURE VANILLA EXTRACT

### TO MAKE THE CAKE

Preheat the oven to 350°F.

Butter an 8- or 9-inch cake pan, and line the bottom with a round of parchment paper, buttering the parchment as well. If you don't have parchment, butter and flour the pan, knocking out the excess flour.

In a double boiler or a metal bowl set over a saucepan of simmering water, melt the chocolate and the butter, stirring until smooth. Set aside to cool slightly. You can also melt them in a microwave, using a microwave-safe bowl and a low setting. Remove the bowl from the microwave frequently, stir, and return it to the microwave, until the chocolate and butter are melted and smooth.

Using an electric mixer, beat the egg yolks with about half the sugar on medium-high speed until pale and thick, about 3 minutes. Fold the chocolate into the egg mixture and set aside.

Wash and dry the beaters. In a clean bowl, beat the egg whites until soft peaks begin to form. With the mixer running, gradually add the remaining sugar and continue beating until medium-firm peaks form, about 5 minutes. Fold the egg whites into the chocolate-yolk mixture in 3 additions.

Put the almond flour, cinnamon, and salt in a fine strainer held over the batter, and sift it into the batter, folding it in in 3 additions.

Pour the batter into the prepared pan. Bake on the middle rack of the oven until a toothpick or knife inserted into the center comes out with only a few crumbs attached, 45 to 50 minutes.

When the cake has cooled completely, run a small knife around the pan sides to loosen it. Invert the cake onto a plate or cooling rack; then invert it again onto a serving plate. Dust with powdered sugar, if desired.

TO MAKE THE WHIPPED CREAM
In an electric mixer on medium-high speed, beat the chilled cream until slightly thickened. Add the sugar and vanilla extract and beat until firm peaks begin to form; do not overbeat.

### TO SERVE
Top each slice of cake with a dollop of whipped cream.

The cake can be made 1 day ahead and stored at room temperature, covered with a dome or with parchment paper and then plastic wrap. It can be refrigerated for up to 2 days and then brought back to room temperature or gently reheated before serving. It is also good served chilled, but the texture will be firmer.

### NOTE
If you can't find toasted almond flour, toast almonds (see page 18) and grind them finely in a food processor or in small batches in a coffee or spice grinder. Sift out any large pieces. You can substitute 1/4 cup all-purpose flour, but the cake will not have the same nutlike flavor.

# BANANA CAKE

SERVES 8 TO 12 / Good as a snack or dessert, this cake is not too sweet and it is loaded with fresh banana flavor. Try it at breakfast or any time of day.

6 TABLESPOONS BUTTER, PLUS MORE
   FOR PAN

3/4 CUP BROWN SUGAR PLUS 1 TABLE-
   SPOON FOR THE TOPPING

3 EGGS

1 TEASPOON PURE VANILLA EXTRACT

3/4 CUP WHOLE-WHEAT FLOUR

3/4 CUP ALL-PURPOSE FLOUR

1 TEASPOON BAKING POWDER

1/2 TEASPOON SALT

1/2 TEASPOON GROUND GINGER

3/4 CUP MILK

1 TABLESPOON FINELY CHOPPED
   CANDIED GINGER (SEE SOURCES)

2 RIPE BANANAS, CUT DIAGONALLY INTO
   THIN SLICES

Preheat the oven to 350°F.

Butter an 8- or 9-inch round cake pan, and line the bottom of the pan with a round of parchment paper. Butter the parchment and dust the pan with flour.

Using an electric mixer, beat the butter and 3/4 cup of the brown sugar until smooth. With the mixer running, add the eggs, one at a time; then add the vanilla extract.

Combine the whole-wheat flour, all-purpose flour, baking powder, salt, and ginger. Add the flour mixture to the batter alternately with the milk, and beat until well combined. Fold in the chopped ginger. Pour half of the batter into the prepared pan, and arrange half of the banana slices in one layer on the batter. Pour the remaining batter into the pan, smoothing it over the banana slices. Arrange the remaining banana slices in a circle on the top of the cake. Sprinkle the remaining tablespoon of brown sugar over the cake, particularly over the banana slices. Bake in the center of the oven until a toothpick or knife inserted into the center comes out clean, 40 to 50 minutes.

Let the cake cool completely, and then run a small knife around the pan sides to loosen it. Carefully invert the cake onto a plate or cooling rack and peel off the parchment. Place a serving plate upside down on top of the cake and invert the cake onto the plate.

# AMARETTO MILK-SOAKED CAKE

**SERVES 9 /** This soft cake is infused with sweet, almond-flavored milk and topped with crisp, crumbled amaretti cookies. It's an impressive dessert, but relatively simple to make—the cake can be baked ahead and bathed in the almond milk before serving. It tastes almost sinfully rich, yet it is relatively low in fat.

## CAKE

4 EGGS, SEPARATED

1/2 CUP SUGAR

1/4 TEASPOON SALT

1/4 TEASPOON PURE VANILLA EXTRACT

1/2 CUP ALL-PURPOSE FLOUR

1/2 CUP TOASTED ALMOND FLOUR
   (SEE NOTES AND SOURCES)

## AMARETTO MILK

1 CUP WHOLE MILK

1 (12-OUNCE) CAN EVAPORATED MILK

3/4 CUP SWEETENED CONDENSED MILK

1 TEASPOON PURE ALMOND EXTRACT

1 TABLESPOON AMARETTO DI SARONNO
   OR OTHER ALMOND-FLAVORED
   LIQUEUR

1 TABLESPOON POWDERED SUGAR

8 AMARETTI COOKIES (EACH ABOUT
   1 INCH IN DIAMETER), PREFERABLY
   LAZZARONI AMARETTI DI SARONNO
   (SEE NOTES AND SOURCES), OR
   16 TO 20 MINI AMARETTI COOKIES,
   CRUMBLED

1 PINT RASPBERRIES (OPTIONAL)

## TO MAKE THE CAKE

Preheat the oven to 350°F. Butter an 8 1/2-inch-square cake pan (see Notes). Line the bottom of the pan with parchment, butter and then flour the parchment, and knock out the excess flour.

Using an electric mixer, beat the egg yolks with half of the sugar, the salt, and vanilla at medium-high speed until pale and fluffy, 3 to 5 minutes. Using a clean, dry bowl and beaters, beat the egg whites, gradually adding the remaining sugar, until soft peaks form, about 5 minutes. Using a large spatula, fold the whites into the yolks in 3 additions. Fold in the sifted flour, 1/4 cup at a time, and then fold in the sifted almond flour, 1/4 cup at a time. (The almond flour may not pass through a fine-mesh strainer; use a coarse strainer if necessary.) Pour the batter into the prepared pan and bake on the middle rack until the cake is golden brown and a toothpick or knife inserted in the center comes out clean, about 30 minutes. Let the cake cool completely. It can be refrigerated in the baking pan, covered tightly with plastic wrap, for up to 1 day.

Invert the cake onto a cutting board. Peel off the parchment and discard. Carefully flip the cake right-side up and, using a sharp, serrated knife, cut away the outer crust on the 4 sides. Cut the cake into thirds, then turn a quarter and make 3 even cuts again, yielding 9 square, evenly sized servings. Carefully place the pieces back in the baking dish (they should fit with a little room around each piece).

(continued on page 133)

In a medium saucepan over medium-high heat, combine the milk and evaporated milk and bring to a simmer. Whisk in the sweetened condensed milk and bring the mixture to a boil. Remove the pot from the heat and stir in the almond extract and amaretto liqueur.

Carefully pour the hot milk mixture into the cake pan without wetting the tops of the cake pieces (you may need to remove one piece and then replace it to do this). Allow the cake to sit for 5 to 10 minutes while it absorbs the milk.

### TO SERVE

Divide the cake among 9 serving plates and spoon the milk remaining in the pan around each piece in a thin layer. Dust the cake with powdered sugar and sprinkle with crumbled amaretti and raspberries, if desired.

The cake is best served warm, but if covered tightly with plastic, it can be refrigerated for up to 1 day. You can bring the cake to room temperature before serving, but it is also good when cold.

### NOTES

You can use a 9-by-13-inch glass baking pan, but reduce the baking time slightly. You can also bake the cake in an 8- or 9-inch round cake pan, in which case you will need a 2- or 3-inch ring mold with which to cut out uniform servings.

If you don't have toasted almond flour, toast almonds (see page 18) and grind them finely in a food processor or in small batches in a coffee or spice grinder. Sift out any large pieces.

Almond biscotti can be substituted for Lazzaroni Amaretti di Saronno cookies, but use only the crisp variety made with no butter or oil.

# CHAPTER 6/
# SIMMERING STEWS AND HOT POTS

**COMMERCIAL BLEND—MILD**
# CURRY POWDER

**KALUSTYAN'S ----- IMPERIAL**
# MILD- CURRY POWDER

**INDIAN — GROUND SPICE MIX**
## TANDOORI MASALA

ZERESHK
SPS 026    4oz

Chicken TIKKA MASALA
0651 SPS    2oz

POULTRY SEASONING
SPS 0041    2oz

**SEA FOOD**
SEASONING

**JAMAICAN**
SEASONING

**ADOBO**
SEASONING

**ITALIAN**
SEASONING

**MID EAST SPICE MIX**
## HAWAIJ

**SPICE MIX FOR**
## FALAFAL

**SPICE FOR**
## LENTIL-SOUP

**SPICE FOR**
## FISH

This chapter is built around the satisfying process of bringing ingredients together in aromatic soups, pastas, vegetable dishes, stews, and desserts. In these recipes, foods and seasonings combine in the saucepan to create rich, powerful flavors. Certain dishes may contain quite a few ingredients, each adding richness to the whole, but don't worry: The preparation is not technically demanding. And although risotto may require some sustained attention, other dishes, such as Couscous with Toasted Almonds and Cumin (page 162) and Polenta with Goat Cheese and Rosemary (page 153), are quite simple to prepare. Stews and soups, as well as vegetable dishes, can cook without your intervention once you have gotten them started.

The pleasure of these recipes is that they are all relatively straightforward. Like the roasted dishes in Chapter 5, these provide the comfort and pleasure one expects from country kitchens, but they are especially friendly to the city cook. They can be made in a small space with minimal equipment, so there will be less workspace clutter and easier cleanup.

In many of the recipes, the primary ingredient is enhanced through the use of a flavorful liquid as the cooking medium. For example, Braised and Caramelized Fennel (page 141) uses a dry white wine, as does Tagine of Red Snapper (page 156), in which saffron and rich stock are infused through slow cooking. In Spaghettini with Veal Meatballs and Chunky Tomato Sauce (page 154), the meatballs simmer in an herbal tomato sauce, and then the pasta is added and allowed to soak up the various flavors.

This process involves more than simply adding liquid to a dish or spooning it over the top. For example, think of the difference between serving a grilled steak with a sauce and simmering cubes of of lamb in fruity pomegranate juice, as in Lamb Stew with Pomegranate and Saffron Fregula (page 160). With the latter, you infuse the sweet and citric elements of the juice into the meat. It's a very intense way of cooking because the flavors totally permeate the food.

Stews and soups, of course, are the quintessential hot pots.

# CAULIFLOWER SOUP WITH GREEN APPLE AND FROMAGE BLANC

**SERVES 6 TO 8 /** When you first taste this elegant soup, it may remind you of vichysoisse, even though the two dishes are quite different. The ingredients here are simple and inexpensive and preparation time is quick, yet the result feels luxurious. (The soup is light, so if you want a bit of extra richness, you can add some heavy cream.) Crisp green apple, as both an ingredient and a garnish, adds a little texture and balances out the creamy cauliflower purée. Serve this soup hot or chilled.

1 TABLESPOON EXTRA-VIRGIN OLIVE OIL

2 TABLESPOONS BUTTER

1 MEDIUM YELLOW ONION, FINELY CHOPPED

2 MEDIUM RIBS CELERY, FINELY CHOPPED

2 LARGE HEADS CAULIFLOWER, FLORETS ONLY, CUT INTO 1-INCH PIECES (ABOUT 2 1/2 POUNDS OF FLORETS, OR 10 CUPS)

7 CUPS CHICKEN STOCK OR CANNED LOW-SODIUM BROTH

2 GRANNY SMITH APPLES

1/2 CUP HEAVY CREAM (OPTIONAL)

2 TEASPOONS FRESHLY SQUEEZED LEMON JUICE

KOSHER SALT

1/2 CUP FROMAGE BLANC (SEE SOURCES), OR SUBSTITUTE CRÈME FRAÎCHE (PAGE 85)

Heat the oil and butter in a large, heavy saucepan over medium heat. Add the onion and celery and cook, stirring occasionally, until the onion is translucent, about 5 minutes. Stir in the cauliflower and cook, stirring, for another 5 minutes. Add the chicken stock and increase the heat to high. When the stock comes to a boil, decrease the heat to medium-low and simmer, covered, for 30 minutes.

Peel, core, and coarsely chop 1 of the apples, add it to the pot, and cook for 1 more minute. Remove the soup from the heat and purée it in batches in a blender. Return the soup to the pot and stir in the heavy cream, if desired, and lemon juice. Season with salt and place over medium heat until just heated through.

Just before serving, halve and core the remaining apple. Cut into very thin slices with a sharp knife, or use a mandoline to shave slices.

Serve the soup in large, shallow bowls, garnished with the shaved apple slices and a dollop of fromage blanc.

# SWEET PEA
# SOUP WITH BASIL AND ALMOND PESTO

SERVES 6 / One of the things I like best about this soup is that it can be served hot or cold. Either way, it is light, refreshing, and evocative of spring. If you choose to make it with vegetable stock, it becomes a totally vegetarian dish. The basil pesto garnish adds bright flavors and crunch to the velvety soup.

## SOUP

2 TABLESPOONS EXTRA-VIRGIN OLIVE
   OIL
1 SMALL ONION, FINELY CHOPPED
2 1/2 POUNDS FROZEN PEAS (FOUR
   10-OUNCE PACKAGES)
ABOUT 5 CUPS CHICKEN OR VEGETABLE
   STOCK OR CANNED LOW-SODIUM
   BROTH
KOSHER SALT
FRESHLY GROUND BLACK PEPPER

## PESTO

1 LARGE BUNCH BASIL, OR ABOUT
   2 1/2 CUPS LOOSELY PACKED LEAVES,
   COARSE STEMS DISCARDED, LEAVES
   WASHED WELL AND SPUN DRY
1/4 CUP CHOPPED BLANCHED ALMONDS
2 TABLESPOONS GRATED PARMESAN
   CHEESE (PREFERABLY PARMIGIANO-
   REGGIANO)
1 1/2 TEASPOONS FRESHLY SQUEEZED
   LEMON JUICE
1/4 CUP EXTRA-VIRGIN OLIVE OIL
KOSHER SALT
FRESHLY GROUND BLACK PEPPER

## TO MAKE THE SOUP

Heat the olive oil in a large saucepan over medium heat and cook the onion, stirring occasionally, until translucent, about 5 minutes. Add the peas and enough stock to cover.

Increase the heat to high and bring the soup to a boil; then decrease the heat and simmer until the peas are just tender, about 5 minutes. Be careful not to overcook, or the peas will lose their bright green color. In batches, purée the soup in a blender, passing each puréed batch through a strainer into a large bowl or other container (use caution; it will be very hot). Season with salt and pepper.

## TO MAKE THE PESTO

In a food processor or blender, combine the basil (reserving a few leaves for garnish), almonds, Parmesan, and lemon juice and process until smooth. Add the olive oil and process to combine. Season with salt and pepper. You should have about 1 1/4 cups. The pesto is best when made and served the same day, but if the surface is covered with plastic wrap, it can be refrigerated for up to 4 days.

## TO SERVE

Serve the soup either hot or chilled. To chill it quickly, place the bowl or container in a larger bowl filled with ice and cold water and let it sit, stirring occasionally, until cool.

Ladle the soup into bowls, top with a dollop of pesto, and garnish with basil leaves.

# BRAISED AND CARAMELIZED FENNEL

**SERVES 4 AS A SIDE DISH** / An early lesson I learned as a chef was how to prepare foods *à l'étuvée*, steamed with butter and slightly caramelized. Here I take the process a step further, adding honey and Riesling to bring out the natural sugars of the crisp vegetable. Fennel done this way tastes almost like fruit and is a great accent to simple fish or poultry dishes.

1 LARGE OR 2 SMALL BULBS FENNEL, FRONDS RESERVED FOR GARNISH

2 TABLESPOONS PLUS 2 TEASPOONS EXTRA-VIRGIN OLIVE OIL

1/2 CUP RIESLING, PINOT BLANC, OR OTHER DRY WHITE WINE

1 CUP WATER

3 TABLESPOONS HONEY

2 TEASPOONS BUTTER (OPTIONAL)

KOSHER SALT

FRESHLY GROUND BLACK PEPPER

Halve the fennel and cut each half into wedges about 1/2 inch thick at the outer edge. Cut out most of the core, but leave enough so that the slices do not fall apart.

Place 2 large, heavy skillets over medium-high heat, and in each heat 1 tablespoon plus 1 teaspoon olive oil (or do this in 1 skillet in batches). Cook the fennel wedges until browned, 3 to 4 minutes on each side. To each skillet add 1/4 cup wine, 1/2 cup water, and 1 1/2 tablespoons honey. When the liquid begins to boil, decrease the heat to medium and simmer until most of the liquid has evaporated and the fennel is tender and glazed, 20 to 30 minutes. If the liquid has reduced too much before the fennel is tender, add a little more water. Add a teaspoon of butter to each pan, if desired, stir, and season with salt and pepper. Transfer the fennel to serving dishes and garnish with the fennel fronds.

# WILD MUSHROOMS
## WITH TRUFFLE BUTTER AND FARRO

SERVES 4 AS A FIRST COURSE OR SIDE DISH / The earthy flavors of this dish work well with a simple braised or grilled main course. Farro, a grain that is southern Italian in origin, has a nutty flavor and chewy texture. It goes well with rustic foods and holds up to sauces—it is not is delicate.

### FARRO

1 TABLESPOON EXTRA-VIRGIN OLIVE OIL

1 SMALL OR $1/2$ LARGE ONION, FINELY CHOPPED

$1^1/2$ CUPS FARRO (SEE SOURCES)

$2^1/2$ CUPS CHICKEN STOCK OR CANNED LOW-SODIUM BROTH

KOSHER SALT

FRESHLY GROUND BLACK PEPPER

### WILD MUSHROOMS

$3/4$ POUND MIXED WILD MUSHROOMS, SUCH AS SHIITAKES, CHANTERELLES, MORELS, OR OYSTER MUSHROOMS

1 TABLESPOON EXTRA-VIRGIN OLIVE OIL

$1/4$ CUP WHITE WINE (SEE NOTE)

1 CUP CHICKEN STOCK OR CANNED LOW-SODIUM BROTH

1 TABLESPOON TRUFFLE BUTTER, OR SUBSTITUTE TRUFFLE OIL (SEE SOURCES)

2 TABLESPOONS COARSELY CHOPPED PARSLEY

KOSHER SALT

FRESHLY GROUND BLACK PEPPER

### TO MAKE THE FARRO

Heat the olive oil in a medium saucepan over medium-high heat and sauté the onion until translucent, 3 to 5 minutes. Add the farro and cook, stirring, until lightly toasted, about 2 minutes. Add the chicken stock and bring to a boil; decrease the heat to medium-low, cover, and simmer until all the liquid has been absorbed, about 30 minutes. Season with salt and pepper.

### TO MAKE THE MUSHROOMS

If using shiitake mushrooms, use the caps only, slicing them $1/2$ inch thick. Use both the caps and stems of other mushrooms, slicing them $1/2$ inch thick if large and leaving smaller mushrooms whole. Heat the olive oil in a large skillet over medium-high heat and sauté the mushrooms until they just begin to brown, 3 to 5 minutes. Decrease the heat to medium. Add the wine and simmer until the liquid has almost evaporated, 2 to 3 minutes. Add the stock and simmer until most of the liquid has evaporated, about 20 minutes. Add the truffle butter and parsley and toss to coat. Season with salt and pepper.

### TO SERVE

Spoon the farro into a large serving bowl and add the mushrooms. Stir to combine.

### NOTE

If you don't have an open bottle of white wine, you can substitute 2 teaspoons of freshly squeezed lemon juice. Add it with the truffle butter and parsley.

# FIVE-SPICE SQUASH PURÉE

**SERVES 6** / Consider this a savory version of pumpkin pie. Smooth, rich, and luxurious, it is excellent with game or poultry and captivating served all by itself. | Cloves, star anise, and, of course, cinnamon can be purchased already ground, but fennel seed and aniseed are usually sold whole. They are easy to grind in a coffee or spice grinder. Any leftover spice mixture will go well with yams or celery root purée or can be rubbed on game before cooking.

## SPICE MIXTURE

1 TABLESPOON FENNEL SEED (SEE SOURCES)

5 OR 6 WHOLE STAR ANISE (SEE SOURCES)

1 TABLESPOON ANISEED (SEE SOURCES)

1 TABLESPOON GROUND CINNAMON

1 TABLESPOON GROUND BLACK PEPPER

1 TABLESPOON GROUND CLOVES

## SQUASH PURÉE

1 LARGE (OR 2 SMALL TO MEDIUM) BUTTERNUT SQUASH, ABOUT 3 1/2 POUNDS

2 TABLESPOONS BUTTER

2 TABLESPOONS MAPLE SYRUP

2 TEASPOONS KOSHER SALT, OR MORE TO TASTE

### TO MAKE THE SPICE MIXTURE

Grind the fennel seed, star anise, and aniseed in a coffee or spice grinder. Combine with the cinnamon, pepper, and cloves and set aside. You should have about 1/3 cup; save any that you have left over, tightly covered, for other uses.

### TO PREPARE THE PURÉE

Preheat the oven to 325°F. Lightly oil a baking sheet with olive oil.

Halve the squash lengthwise and remove and discard the seeds. Place the squash cut-side down on the baking sheet and roast until it is soft and easily pierced with a knife, 40 to 50 minutes. Allow the squash to cool for 15 minutes. Using a large spoon, scoop out the flesh and transfer to a blender. Add the butter, maple syrup, and salt, and process until smooth. Add 1 teaspoon of the spice mixture and blend. Add additional salt or spice mixture to taste.

# RISOTTO
## WITH CHANTERELLES AND PINE NUTS

**SERVES 4** / This is one of my favorite risottos because it showcases the flavor of great chanterelles and the crisp texture of toasted pine nuts. The dish is good served all alone as a light lunch or as a side dish with a simple grilled or roasted meat.

8 OUNCES FRESH CHANTERELLES,
  STEMS TRIMMED

3 TABLESPOONS EXTRA-VIRGIN OLIVE
  OIL

KOSHER SALT

FRESHLY GROUND BLACK PEPPER

ABOUT 6 CUPS CHICKEN STOCK OR
  CANNED LOW-SODIUM BROTH

1 SHALLOT, FINELY CHOPPED

1 1/2 CUPS ARBORIO RICE

1/2 CUP DRY WHITE WINE

2 TABLESPOONS FRESHLY GRATED
  PARMIGIANO-REGGIANO CHEESE PLUS
  1/2 CUP LOOSELY PACKED SHAVED
  PARMIGIANO-REGGIANO

1/2 CUP PINE NUTS, TOASTED (PAGE 18)

2 TABLESPOONS COARSELY CHOPPED
  FLAT-LEAF PARSLEY

Halve the chanterelles lengthwise if they are large; leave small ones whole. In a medium skillet over medium-high heat, heat 1 tablespoon of the olive oil and sauté the mushrooms until tender, 3 to 4 minutes. Season with salt and pepper and set aside.

In a medium saucepan over medium heat, bring the chicken stock to a gentle simmer.

Heat the remaining 2 tablespoons olive oil in a large, heavy pot over medium-high heat and cook the shallot, stirring occasionally, until translucent, 3 to 5 minutes. Add the rice and cook, stirring, to coat the grains with oil and lightly toast them. Add the wine and cook, stirring frequently, until most of the liquid has been absorbed, 6 to 7 minutes. Begin adding stock, about 1 cup at a time, allowing the rice to absorb the liquid before adding more. Cook, stirring frequently, until the rice is tender but al dente, about 20 minutes.

You may not need to use all of the chicken stock. If you need more liquid, add stock or water. Add the grated Parmigiano-Reggiano, sautéed mushrooms, pine nuts, and parsley to the rice and stir to combine. Season with salt and pepper, garnish with the shaved Parmigiano-Reggiano, and serve.

# LOBSTER AND CORN RISOTTO WITH BASIL-CILANTRO OIL

SERVES 4 / You will think of summer when you see this colorful risotto and inhale its aromas of the sea and garden. This light, healthful combination always puts me in a sunny, warm-weather mood. | To blanch the basil and cilantro, hold each herb bunch by the stems, as you would hold a bunch of flowers, and dunk it first in the boiling water and then in the ice water. You may lose a few leaves, but this method is much easier than trying to quickly fish a large quantity of free-floating herbs out of the water.

### BASIL-CILANTRO OIL

1 LARGE BUNCH BASIL

1 LARGE BUNCH CILANTRO

3/4 CUP EXTRA-VIRGIN OLIVE OIL

1/2 TEASPOON FRESHLY SQUEEZED
    LEMON JUICE

KOSHER SALT

FRESHLY GROUND BLACK PEPPER

### LOBSTER AND CORN RISOTTO

2 LIVE LOBSTERS, 1 1/4 TO 1 1/2 POUNDS
    EACH

2 EARS CORN

2 TABLESPOONS EXTRA-VIRGIN OLIVE
    OIL

ABOUT 5 CUPS CHICKEN STOCK OR
    CANNED LOW-SODIUM BROTH

1 SMALL ONION, FINELY CHOPPED

1 1/2 CUPS ARBORIO RICE

3/4 CUP WHITE WINE

3 TABLESPOONS FRESHLY GRATED
    PARMIGIANO-REGGIANO CHEESE

KOSHER SALT

FRESHLY GROUND BLACK PEPPER

2 TABLESPOONS FRESHLY SQUEEZED
    LIME JUICE

2 TABLESPOONS FINELY CHOPPED
    CILANTRO

4 BASIL SPRIGS

### TO MAKE THE OIL

Bring a large pot of water to a boil. Fill a large bowl with ice water and set aside. Blanch the basil and cilantro in the boiling water for about 20 seconds and then cool immediately in the ice water.

Dry the herbs, remove the coarse stems, and put the leaves and thinner stems in a blender. Add the oil and lemon juice and process until smooth. Season with salt and pepper. The oil can be refrigerated, covered, for up to 3 days; return to room temperature before using. You should have about 1 1/2 cups. Any leftover oil can be drizzled on grilled chicken or fish or stirred into rice or pasta.

### TO COOK THE LOBSTERS

Bring a very large pot of heavily salted water to a boil. Fill a very large bowl with ice water and set aside.

Put the lobsters into the boiling water head first and cook for 6 to 8 minutes, then plunge into the ice water to stop the cooking. When the lobsters are cool, remove the meat from the tails, claws, and knuckles and discard the shells. Cut the tail meat and large parts of the claw meat into bite-sized pieces. The lobster meat can be refrigerated, covered, for up to 6 hours.

### TO MAKE THE RISOTTO

Bring a large pot of unsalted water to a boil and cook the corn for 5 minutes (salt in the water would toughen the tender skins on the kernels). Remove the corn from the water and allow it to cool (or cool the corn in the same bowl of ice water you used for the lobsters). Break the cobs in half. Using a sharp knife, cut the kernels from the cobs. You should have about 1 1/2 cups of kernels. Reserve the kernels and the cobs.

(continued on next page)

Heat 1 tablespoon of the olive oil in a medium saucepan over medium-high heat. Add the corncobs and saute to brown slightly, about 5 minutes (they will add rich flavor to the stock). Add the chicken stock and bring to a boil; decrease the heat to low and keep the stock at a simmer.

In a medium saucepan over medium-high heat, heat the remaining tablespoon of olive oil and cook the onion, stirring occasionally, until translucent, 3 to 5 minutes. Add the rice and cook, stirring, to coat the grains with oil and lightly toast. Add the wine and cook, stirring frequently, until most of the liquid has been absorbed, about 5 minutes. Begin adding stock, about 1 cup at a time, allowing the rice to absorb it before adding more, and stirring frequently.

Cook until the rice is al dente, about 20 minutes. You may not need to use all of the chicken stock. If you need to use more liquid, add water or additional stock (discarding the corncobs). Stir in the Parmigiano-Reggiano and season with salt and pepper. Add the reserved lobster pieces and corn kernels and cook to warm through. Stir in the lime juice and cilantro and reseason.

### TO SERVE

Spoon the risotto onto plates or into shallow bowls, drizzle with the basil-cilantro oil, and garnish with basil sprigs.

# COCONUT RISOTTO CAKES

SERVES 4 / These creamy cakes are the perfect accompaniment to Miso-Grilled Tuna (page 95). If you prefer to make them with less wine, substitute a cup or two of additional water or stock for the same amount of wine.

1 TABLESPOON PLUS 1 TEASPOON
    EXTRA-VIRGIN OLIVE OIL

1 TABLESPOON FINELY CHOPPED PEELED
    FRESH GINGER

1 CUP ARBORIO RICE

3 CUPS SAKE OR WHITE WINE

ABOUT 2 CUPS HOT WATER OR CHICKEN
    STOCK OR CANNED LOW-SODIUM
    BROTH

1/2 CUP UNSWEETENED CANNED
    COCONUT MILK

1/4 CUP PINE NUTS, TOASTED (PAGE 18)
    AND COARSELY CHOPPED

2 SCALLIONS, WHITE AND ABOUT
    3 INCHES OF GREEN, THINLY SLICED

1 TABLESPOON FINELY CHOPPED
    CILANTRO

KOSHER SALT

FRESHLY GROUND PEPPER

2 CUPS PANKO CRUMBS (SEE SOURCES)

3 TO 4 TABLESPOONS GRAPESEED OIL
    OR OTHER NEUTRAL OIL, SUCH AS
    CANOLA

Heat the olive oil in a medium saucepan over medium-high heat and cook the ginger, stirring, for 1 to 2 minutes. Add the rice and stir for 1 to 2 minutes to lightly toast the grains. Add 1 cup of the sake and continue stirring. As the rice absorbs the liquid, add the remaining sake, 1 cup at a time. When most of the liquid has been absorbed, begin adding hot water, 1 cup at a time, until the grains are tender, about 40 minutes. Allow the risotto to cool for about 10 minutes.

Stir the coconut milk, pine nuts, scallions, and cilantro into the risotto. Season with salt and pepper, spread the risotto evenly on a baking sheet or in a shallow baking dish, and refrigerate until chilled. (It can be made to this point up to 1 day ahead.)

Transfer the chilled risotto to a mixing bowl and stir in 1/2 cup of the panko crumbs. Season with more salt, if necessary. Form the risotto into cakes about 3/4 inch thick; if the mixture is too soft to form, add more panko crumbs. Spread the remaining panko crumbs in a shallow dish or plate and coat each cake with the crumbs.

In a large skillet over medium-high heat, heat 3 to 4 tablespoons of grapeseed oil and cook the risotto cakes until golden brown and crisp, 3 to 4 minutes on each side. Keep the cakes warm in a 200°F oven until ready to serve.

# CREAMY TAGLIATELLE
## WITH ROASTED RADICCHIO AND SHAVED ASIAGO

SERVES 6 / Sarah Wilson, who was the chef at my restaurant Commissary, in Portland, Maine, created this hearty, wintry dish. I find it to be equally comforting in a big city chill. With the crunch of walnuts and the smokiness of radicchio, it is a complex and satisfying pasta.

1 LARGE OR 2 SMALL HEADS RADICCHIO, CORED AND THE LEAVES SEPARATED

5 TABLESPOONS EXTRA-VIRGIN OLIVE OIL

KOSHER SALT

FRESHLY GROUND BLACK PEPPER

8 CLOVES GARLIC, PEELED AND HALVED LENGTHWISE (ABOUT 2 OUNCES)

1/2 CUP PLUS 2 TABLESPOONS VEGETABLE OR CHICKEN STOCK OR CANNED LOW-SODIUM BROTH

1 1/2 CUPS HEAVY CREAM

3 TABLESPOONS GRATED LEMON ZEST

1 POUND TAGLIATELLE, SPINACH TAGLIATELLE, OR ANY LONG, FLAT PASTA

4 CUPS LOOSELY PACKED BABY ARUGULA LEAVES, BABY SPINACH, OR COARSELY CHOPPED ARUGULA

3 OUNCES SHAVED ASIAGO CHEESE (ABOUT 1 CUP LOOSELY PACKED)

1/2 CUP WALNUTS, TOASTED (PAGE 18) AND COARSELY CHOPPED

Preheat the oven to 250°F.

In a large bowl, toss the radicchio leaves with 3 tablespoons of the oil and season with salt and pepper.

Line a baking sheet with parchment, place the radicchio on it, and roast until softened and slightly browned, about 5 minutes. Watch carefully so the leaves do not burn. Remove from the oven and transfer to a plate.

In a medium skillet over low heat, heat the remaining 2 tablespoons oil and cook the garlic cloves until softened and lightly golden, 15 to 20 minutes. Using a slotted spoon, remove the garlic. In a food processor, purée the garlic with 2 tablespoons of the stock. (A miniprocessor works best for these small quantities, or use a mortar and pestle to mash the garlic and stock into a paste.)

In a medium saucepan over high heat, bring the cream to a boil. Decrease the heat and simmer until reduced by half, 30 to 40 minutes. Whisk in the garlic purée, the remaining 1/2 cup stock, and the lemon zest and season with salt and pepper.

Bring a large pot of salted water to a boil over high heat and cook the pasta until al dente. Drain the pasta well and return to the pot. Add the cream sauce, radicchio, and arugula leaves and half of the shaved Asiago and toss to coat well. (This may seem like a lot of arugula, but it will quickly wilt from the heat of the pasta.) Serve the pasta in large bowls topped with the remaining shaved Asiago and the chopped walnuts.

# FARRO PASTA
## WITH CHICKEN, TOMATO, BASIL, AND PISTACHIOS

SERVES 4 / When I served dinner to a health-conscious guest—a personal trainer—I put this dish together on the spur of the moment, using ingredients I had in the kitchen. (If your kitchen doesn't stock farro pasta or fennel pollen, you can find them online.) It was a total success, light and delicious, with an attractive mix of textures. | Sprinkle fennel pollen over food the way you would salt or pepper. A popular seasoning in Italy, it adds the essence of fennel to foods.

1 POUND FARRO PASTA IN ANY SHORT SHAPE, SUCH AS PENNE (SEE SOURCES), OR SUBSTITUTE WHOLE-WHEAT PASTA

2 OUNCES PANCETTA, DICED

3 BONELESS, SKINLESS CHICKEN BREASTS, ABOUT 1½ POUNDS TOTAL, CUT INTO THIN STRIPS

KOSHER SALT

FRESHLY GROUND BLACK PEPPER

1 TABLESPOON FENNEL POLLEN (SEE SOURCES)

PINCH OF DRIED HOT RED PEPPER FLAKES

½ CUP WHITE WINE

4 MEDIUM VINE-RIPENED TOMATOES OR 6 PLUM TOMATOES, CUT INTO LARGE DICE

4 CUPS LOOSELY PACKED BABY SPINACH

2 OUNCES MANCHEGO CHEESE, SHAVED, OR SUBSTITUTE ANOTHER FIRM, MILD SPANISH CHEESE

½ CUP LOOSELY PACKED BASIL LEAVES, COARSELY TORN, PLUS A FEW EXTRA LEAVES FOR GARNISH

¾ CUP PISTACHIO NUTS, TOASTED (PAGE 18) AND COARSELY CHOPPED

Bring a large pot of salted water to a boil over high heat and cook the pasta until al dente. Drain the pasta well and return to the pot, reserving ½ cup of the cooking water.

While the pasta is cooking, heat a large skillet over medium-high heat and brown the pancetta slightly, 2 to 3 minutes. Season the chicken with salt, pepper, and fennel pollen, and add it to the pan. Sprinkle with the dried red pepper flakes. Cook for 2 to 3 minutes, add the wine, and cook for another 2 to 3 minutes, scraping any browned bits from the bottom of the pan and allowing the wine to reduce by about three quarters. Add the tomatoes and cook for 2 to 3 minutes more. Add the chicken mixture and its cooking liquid to the pasta. Add the spinach and toss to wilt and combine well. If the mixture is dry, add some of the reserved pasta-cooking water. Add the cheese, basil, and pistachios and toss to combine. Season with salt and pepper, garnish with basil leaves, and serve.

# ORECCHIETTE
## WITH FRESH PEAS AND GOAT CHEESE

SERVES 4 / The sauce for this pasta is relatively light, yet it tastes rich and creamy, thanks to the flavorful concentrated stock and the tangy goat cheese. | If you don't have fresh peas, do not substitute frozen! Instead, try broccoli florets, zucchini, or any other fresh green vegetable, blanched until crisp-tender. If you like, you may use your favorite herbal accent, such as mint, basil, marjoram, or rosemary.

5 CUPS CHICKEN STOCK OR CANNED
    LOW-SODIUM BROTH, PLUS MORE,
    IF NEEDED
8 OUNCES SOFT GOAT CHEESE,
    CRUMBLED
KOSHER SALT, IF NEEDED
1 POUND ORECCHIETTE PASTA, OR
    SUBSTITUTE FUSILLI
2 POUNDS FRESH PEAS, TO YIELD
    2 CUPS SHELLED PEAS
3 TABLESPOONS FINELY CHOPPED
    SUMMER SAVORY, OR SUBSTITUTE
    ANOTHER HERB TO TASTE
FRESHLY GROUND BLACK PEPPER

Put the chicken stock in a large sauté pan over medium-high heat and bring to a boil. Cook until reduced by half, 15 to 20 minutes. Add the goat cheese and whisk to thoroughly combine. Taste for seasoning—you may not need to add any salt, depending on the saltiness of both the stock and the goat cheese.

Bring a large pot of salted water to a boil over high heat and cook the pasta until al dente. Drain the pasta. If your sauté pan is large enough, add the pasta to the sauce; if it is not, return the pasta to its cooking pot and pour the sauce over it. Add the peas (they do not need to be blanched first). Place the mixture over very low heat, stir to combine, and cook until the pasta has absorbed some of the sauce and the peas are heated through, 2 to 3 minutes. If the pasta absorbs most of the sauce or looks dry, add a little more chicken stock.

Stir in the chopped herbs, season with ground pepper, and serve immediately.

NOTE

This is a versatile sauce. You can add sautéed sliced chicken breast to the pasta, or use the sauce on its own over grilled chicken or tossed with steamed or blanched vegetables. With the addition of fresh mint, it becomes an excellent sauce for roasted lamb or grilled lamb chops.

# POLENTA
## WITH GOAT CHEESE AND ROSEMARY

SERVES 6 / If you like polenta enriched with generous amounts of cream, butter, or cheese, try this lighter version instead, for a healthful but still delicious change. It is smooth and comforting, with the tangy flavor of goat cheese, and it makes a perfect companion to Coriander-Crusted Pork Loin Stuffed with Dried Peaches and Pine Nuts (page 126).

6 CUPS WATER

KOSHER SALT

2 CUPS POLENTA (STONE-GROUND
    YELLOW CORNMEAL)

6 OUNCES SOFT GOAT CHEESE,
    CRUMBLED

1 TEASPOON FINELY CHOPPED
    ROSEMARY

2 TABLESPOONS BUTTER (OPTIONAL)

FRESHLY GROUND BLACK PEPPER

In a heavy, medium saucepan over high heat, bring the water and 1 teaspoon salt to a boil. Whisk in the polenta in a steady stream. Decrease the heat to medium and cook, stirring with a wooden spoon, until the polenta begins to thicken, about 10 minutes. Stir in the goat cheese and rosemary and continue cooking for another 1 to 2 minutes. Stir in the butter, if desired. Season with salt and pepper.

Keep the polenta covered until ready to serve. It will continue to thicken as it sits, so you may want to cook it to a slightly thinner consistency if it will wait more than a few minutes.

# SPAGHETTINI
## WITH VEAL MEATBALLS AND CHUNKY TOMATO SAUCE

SERVES 4 TO 6 / Here is fragrant, satisfying comfort food at its best. The all-time favorite, meatballs and spaghetti, is lightened with veal and dressed up with fresh herbs and a touch of cream and nutmeg. Make it a day or two before serving and it will taste even better, intensifying in flavor as it waits. | Start the Chunky Tomato Sauce (recipe follows) at least an hour before preparing the meatballs, since it needs simmering time. Or make it ahead and refrigerate.

2 TABLESPOONS BUTTER

1 MEDIUM ONION, FINELY CHOPPED

1 TABLESPOON MINCED GARLIC

1 1/2 POUNDS GROUND VEAL

2 TABLESPOONS BREAD CRUMBS

2 TEASPOONS FINELY CHOPPED FRESH TARRAGON

1/2 CUP FINELY CHOPPED FLAT-LEAF PARSLEY, PLUS ADDITIONAL FOR GARNISH

1/4 TEASPOON FRESHLY GRATED NUTMEG

2 EGGS, LIGHTLY BEATEN

1/2 CUP FRESHLY GRATED PARMIGIANO-REGGIANO CHEESE (ABOUT 2 OUNCES), PLUS ADDITIONAL FOR GARNISH

1/4 CUP HEAVY CREAM

2 TEASPOONS KOSHER SALT

1 TEASPOON FRESHLY GROUND BLACK PEPPER

EXTRA-VIRGIN OLIVE OIL FOR SAUTÉING MEATBALLS

CHUNKY TOMATO SAUCE (RECIPE FOLLOWS)

1 POUND SPAGHETTINI, SPAGHETTI, LINGUINE, OR OTHER LONG, THIN PASTA

In a large skillet over medium heat, melt the butter and cook the onion and garlic, stirring occasionally, until the onion is translucent, about 5 minutes. Transfer the onion and garlic to a large mixing bowl and wipe out the skillet with a paper towel.

To the cooked onion and garlic, add the veal, bread crumbs, tarragon, parsley, nutmeg, egg, Parmigiano-Reggiano, and cream. Season with salt and pepper and mix well. Shape the mixture into 1 1/2-inch balls.

In the same large skillet over medium-high heat, heat just enough oil to cover the bottom of the pan, and brown the meatballs on all sides, cooking them in batches to avoid overcrowding. Drain on paper towels. Return all the meatballs to the skillet and add the Chunky Tomato Sauce (or add the meatballs to the large pot of sauce), and simmer for 30 minutes.

While the meatballs and sauce are simmering, make the spaghettini. Bring a large pot of salted water to a boil and cook the spaghettini until al dente. Drain the pasta and return it to the cooking pot. Add a large spoonful or two of the tomato sauce to the pasta and toss to coat (to prevent sticking). Divide the pasta among 4 to 6 serving plates. Top with the sauce and meatballs, and sprinkle with grated Parmigiano-Reggiano and chopped parsley.

# CHUNKY TOMATO SAUCE

**MAKES 8 CUPS** / You can achieve the rough texture that gives tomato sauce its homespun appeal only when you make your own. It is easy to do and requires very little in the way of technique or expertise. Use this sauce for your favorite pasta, with or without meatballs, or spoon it over Cheddar Meatloaf (page 122).

2 TABLESPOONS EXTRA-VIRGIN OLIVE
OIL
1 MEDIUM YELLOW ONION, FINELY
CHOPPED
2 TABLESPOONS FINELY CHOPPED
GARLIC
3 (28-OUNCE) CANS PLUM TOMATOES
2 TABLESPOONS SUGAR
1 TABLESPOON PLUS 1 TEASPOON FINELY
CHOPPED FRESH THYME
1 1/2 TABLESPOONS FINELY CHOPPED
FRESH OREGANO OR MARJORAM, OR
A COMBINATION OF BOTH
KOSHER SALT
FRESHLY GROUND BLACK PEPPER

Heat the olive oil in a large pot over medium heat. Add the onion and garlic and cook, stirring occasionally, until the onion is translucent, about 5 minutes.

Crush the tomatoes by hand so that they are still somewhat chunky, and add them, with their juice, to the pot. Add the sugar, thyme, and oregano. Bring to a boil; decrease the heat and simmer until the sauce reaches the desired thickness, about 1 hour. Season well with salt and pepper. The sauce can be refrigerated for up to 3 days or frozen for up to 2 months.

# TAGINE OF RED SNAPPER

SERVES 4 / A tagine, the Moroccan version of a stew, is named for the heavy pottery dish with a cone-shaped lid in which it is traditionally cooked. But you can make an authentic tagine in your own large pan, as long as it is heavy and straight-sided and has a tight-fitting lid. | Everything is cooked in a single pan, and the flavors of the artichoke hearts, potatoes, lemons, and tomatoes combine to create an exotic, one-dish meal. Serve it with crusty bread for soaking up the sauce.

4 PLUM TOMATOES

2 LEMONS

2 ARTICHOKES

1 SMALL BULB FENNEL

2 CUPS CHICKEN OR VEGETABLE STOCK OR CANNED LOW-SODIUM BROTH

1 TEASPOON SAFFRON THREADS

1 CUP FLOUR

1$^1$/2 POUNDS RED SNAPPER FILLETS, CUT INTO 3-OUNCE PIECES, SKIN REMOVED (THE FISHMONGER CAN DO THIS)

KOSHER SALT

FRESHLY GROUND BLACK PEPPER

2 TABLESPOONS EXTRA-VIRGIN OLIVE OIL

$^1$/2 POUND SMALL FINGERLING POTATOES, UNPEELED, SLICED LENGTHWISE $^1$/4 INCH THICK

$^3$/4 CUP WHITE WINE

$^1$/3 CUP LOOSELY PACKED CILANTRO LEAVES

Bring a large pot of salted water to a boil. Fill a large bowl with ice and water.

With a small, sharp paring knife, cut away the stem end of each tomato and cut an X at the bottom. Blanch the tomatoes in the boiling water for 1 to 2 minutes, remove them using a slotted spoon, and plunge them into the ice water. Drain and peel, discarding the skins. Quarter each tomato lengthwise, and cut the quarters in half. Set aside.

Halve one of the lemons and squeeze the juice into a large nonreactive bowl. Add the squeezed lemon halves to the bowl, and fill it with water.

Cut off each artichoke stem and, starting at the base, snap off the tough outer leaves. Using a small, sharp knife, trim around the base of the artichoke until no dark green areas remain. Cut away all the tender leaves, leaving just the artichoke bottom. Using a small spoon, scoop out the choke, leaving the artichoke heart. Quarter the artichoke hearts and immediately put them into the lemon water, to prevent discoloration.

Halve the fennel and place the halves cut-side down on a cutting board. Starting at the base and cutting at a 45-degree angle, cut the halves into $^1$/4-inch-thick semicircles.

In a small pan over medium heat, combine the stock and the saffron and bring to a simmer. Decrease the heat to low and allow the stock to simmer gently while you complete the recipe.

Spread the flour on a small plate. Season the snapper pieces with salt and pepper and dredge in the flour.

In a large, heavy, straight-sided pan over medium-high heat, heat the olive oil and add the snapper pieces. Add the potato slices, artichoke hearts, and fennel and cook for 2 to 3 minutes, lifting the snapper with a spatula so that it doesn't stick to the pan.

Quarter and seed the remaining lemon and add it to the pan; add the tomatoes. Cook for 1 minute, then add the wine and cook until the wine is reduced by two thirds, 7 to 8 minutes. Add the stock, decrease the heat to medium, and simmer, covered, for about 5 minutes. Uncover the pan and simmer for another 5 to 7 minutes. Remove the lemon pieces and add the cilantro.

Divide the fish and vegetables among 4 warmed plates or shallow soup bowls, spooning the liquid over the top.

# OSSO BUCO
## WITH DRIED ORANGE, THYME, AND WHITE BEANS

SERVES 4 / Traditional osso buco is a braised dish that combines the simple flavors of veal, wine, and vegetables. In my version, candied orange zest adds complexity to the classic flavors and textures. I like osso buco best when it is served with white beans, but it is also excellent with risotto or other grains.

### BEANS

2 CUPS DRIED WHITE CANNELLINI BEANS

6 TO 8 CUPS CHICKEN STOCK, CANNED LOW-SODIUM BROTH, OR WATER

1/2 MEDIUM CARROT, PEELED AND CUT IN HALF

1/2 RIB CELERY

KOSHER SALT

1 TEASPOON CHOPPED FRESH THYME

2 TABLESPOONS DICED CANDIED ORANGE PEEL

FRESHLY GROUND BLACK PEPPER

### OSSO BUCO

3 TABLESPOONS EXTRA-VIRGIN OLIVE OIL

4 VEAL SHANKS, ABOUT 2 INCHES THICK, 1 TO 1 1/4 POUNDS EACH

KOSHER SALT

FRESHLY GROUND BLACK PEPPER

1 MEDIUM ONION, COARSELY CHOPPED

2 MEDIUM CARROTS, 1 COARSELY CHOPPED AND 1 CUT INTO 1/4-INCH DICE

2 RIBS CELERY, 1 COARSELY CHOPPED AND 1 CUT INTO 1/4-INCH DICE

2 CUPS WHITE WINE

8 CUPS VEAL STOCK, OR SUBSTITUTE CHICKEN STOCK OR CANNED LOW-SODIUM BROTH

6 SPRIGS FRESH THYME

2 TABLESPOONS DICED CANDIED ORANGE PEEL

### TO MAKE THE BEANS

Place the beans in a bowl, cover with water by about 3 inches, and set aside to soak overnight or up to 24 hours. Refrigerate if the kitchen is very warm.

Drain and rinse the soaked beans and put them in a medium saucepan over medium heat with 6 cups of the chicken stock, the carrot, and the celery. Cover and bring to a boil. Decrease the heat to medium-low and simmer gently until tender, about 1 hour, adding more chicken stock or water if needed to keep the beans fully covered. Add salt just before the beans are fully cooked (the skins will crack if it is added too early).

Drain the beans and return them to the same pot, discarding the carrot and celery. Add the thyme and orange peel and mix gently. Season with salt and pepper.

If you prefer not to soak the beans overnight, cook as described above, but you will need at least 8 cups of liquid and the beans will take at least 2 hours to cook. The beans can be fully cooked up to 2 days ahead, refrigerated in their cooking liquid, and brought back to a simmer before proceeding with the recipe.

### TO MAKE THE OSSO BUCO

In a large, heavy pot over medium-high heat, heat 2 tablespoons of the oil. Season the veal shanks with salt and pepper and add to the pot. Add the onion, coarsely chopped carrot, and coarsely chopped celery and brown the shanks for 3 to 5 minutes per side.

Add the wine and stir with a wooden spoon, scraping up any browned bits from the bottom of the pot. Cook until the wine is reduced to about 1/2 cup, 5 to 7 minutes. Add the veal stock and 2 sprigs of the thyme and bring to a boil. Decrease the heat to medium, cover, and simmer until the meat is very tender and the braising liquid has reduced by half, about 1 hour and 40 minutes. If the liquid is reducing too much during cooking, add water.

Remove the veal shanks and set aside, loosely covered with foil. Strain the braising liquid and reserve; discard the solids.

In a large, heavy skillet, heat the remaining tablespoon of oil over medium heat. Add the diced carrot and diced celery and cook until softened but not browned, about 5 minutes. Add the braising liquid. If the sauce is too thick, add chicken stock or water to thin it. Simmer for about 1 minute to heat through, or longer if the vegetables are not fully cooked, and season with salt and pepper.

TO SERVE

Divide the beans among 4 warmed plates. Top with the veal shanks, spoon the sauce over them, and garnish with the diced orange peel and remaining thyme sprigs.

# LAMB STEW
## WITH POMEGRANATE AND SAFFRON FREGULA

SERVES 4 / The fruity flavors of pomegranate and orange, along with saffron, toasted cumin, cayenne, and ginger, infuse the lamb as it cooks. Pomegranate contrasts with the rich lamb broth and helps to make the stew very pretty on the plate. | Fregula is a kind of Sardinian couscous. When cooked, it plumps up like corn. It has a nutty flavor and is great with stews, as well as by itself.

### LAMB STEW

2 TABLESPOONS EXTRA-VIRGIN OLIVE OIL, PLUS MORE IF NEEDED

1 1/2 POUNDS LAMB SHOULDER, TRIMMED AND CUT INTO 1-INCH CHUNKS

KOSHER SALT

FRESHLY GROUND BLACK PEPPER

1 LARGE CARROT, CUT INTO ABOUT 3/4-INCH DICE

2 SHALLOTS, ROUGHLY CHOPPED

1 TEASPOON GROUND CUMIN

1/2 TEASPOON CAYENNE PEPPER

2 TEASPOONS FINELY CHOPPED PEELED FRESH GINGER

2 CUPS POMEGRANATE JUICE (SEE SOURCES), OR 1 CUP RED WINE

PINCH OF SAFFRON THREADS

5 CUPS CHICKEN STOCK OR CANNED LOW-SODIUM BROTH

1 TABLESPOON FINELY CHOPPED ORANGE ZEST

2 TABLESPOONS POMEGRANATE MOLASSES (SEE NOTE AND SOURCES)

### SAFFRON FREGULA

3 CUPS CHICKEN STOCK OR CANNED LOW-SODIUM BROTH

1 TEASPOON SAFFRON THREADS

KOSHER SALT

1 1/2 CUPS FREGULA (SEE SOURCES), OR SUBSTITUTE ISRAELI COUSCOUS

1/4 CUP COARSELY CHOPPED FRESH MINT

1/2 CUP POMEGRANATE SEEDS (OPTIONAL)

### TO MAKE THE STEW

In a large, heavy pot over medium-high heat, heat 2 tablespoons olive oil. Season the lamb pieces with salt and pepper and brown on all sides in the oil, working in batches if necessary, so they are not crowded, 6 to 8 minutes per batch. Using a slotted spoon, transfer the lamb to a bowl. Add 1 tablespoon or more of oil to the pot, if necessary, and sauté the carrot for 2 to 3 minutes. Add the shallots, cumin, cayenne, and ginger and sauté for another 2 to 3 minutes to toast the spices. Add the pomegranate juice and saffron. Scrape up any browned bits on the bottom of the pot. If using pomegranate juice, cook until reduced to about 1/2 cup, 15 to 20 minutes, and if using red wine, cook until reduced to about 1/4 cup, 8 to 10 minutes. Return the lamb and any juices to the pot, add the chicken stock and orange zest, and bring to a boil. Decrease the heat to medium-low and cook, covered, for about 1/2 hour, removing the cover to skim the liquid occasionally and to make sure that the stew remains at a gentle simmer. Uncover and cook for another hour, or until the lamb is tender and the liquid has thickened. Add the pomegranate molasses and season with salt and pepper.

### TO MAKE THE FREGULA

In a medium saucepan over high heat, combine the chicken stock and the saffron. If using low-sodium chicken broth, add 2 teaspoons salt. Bring to a boil and add the fregula. Decrease the heat to low and cook, covered, until the liquid is absorbed, 25 to 30 minutes. Season with salt.

Divide the fregula among 4 bowls and top with stew. Garnish with mint and pomegranate seeds, if desired.

### NOTE

Depending upon the richness of the stock, you may want to use more or less pomegranate molasses, so add 1 tablespoon at a time and taste after each addition.

# COUSCOUS
## WITH TOASTED ALMONDS AND CUMIN

SERVES 4 / You can create dozens of variations on couscous, depending on the herb, nut, or spice you choose as an accent. This semolina product is traditional with fish or lamb, but it is good with any dish that has extra sauce to be soaked up by the fluffy grains.

2 1/4 CUPS CHICKEN STOCK OR CANNED
   LOW-SODIUM BROTH
2 TABLESPOONS EXTRA-VIRGIN OLIVE
   OIL
1 TABLESPOON PLUS 1 TEASPOON
   FRESHLY SQUEEZED LEMON JUICE
1 1/2 TEASPOONS GROUND CUMIN
1 1/2 CUPS INSTANT COUSCOUS
KOSHER SALT
1/3 CUP SLIVERED ALMONDS, TOASTED
   (PAGE 18), OR TOASTED CHOPPED
   ALMONDS
FRESHLY GROUND BLACK PEPPER

In a medium saucepan over high heat, bring the chicken stock, olive oil, lemon juice, and cumin to a boil. Stir in the couscous. If using canned low-sodium chicken broth, add a teaspoon of salt to the stock. Immediately remove the pan from the heat, cover, and let stand for 15 minutes. Fluff the couscous with a fork, stir in the almonds, and season with salt and pepper.

# WARM ARBORIO RICE PUDDING WITH VANILLA AND COCONUT

SERVES 6 / Rice pudding is homey and comforting, but in this version it is light and refined as well. Because the pudding is made with starchy arborio rice and no eggs, it resembles a risotto more than it does a custard, with the grains of rice remaining separate and the flavors of coconut and vanilla coming through clearly. Serve it with your favorite thin wafers or crisp lace cookies or with sliced fresh strawberries.

1 CUP ARBORIO RICE

2 1/2 CUPS WATER

PINCH OF SALT

1 CUP PLUS 2 TABLESPOONS PALM SUGAR (SEE SOURCES), OR SUBSTITUTE 1 CUP GRANULATED WHITE SUGAR

1/2 VANILLA BEAN, SPLIT LENGTHWISE

2 (14-OUNCE) CANS UNSWEETENED COCONUT MILK

1/4 CUP HEAVY CREAM (OPTIONAL)

1 TABLESPOON GRATED LIME ZEST (OPTIONAL)

In a medium, heavy saucepan over high heat, combine the rice, water, salt, and sugar. Scrape the seeds from the vanilla bean into the pot and add the pod. Stir continuously until the water comes to a boil; then decrease the heat to medium-low and cook, stirring frequently, until reduced by half, about 20 minutes. Begin adding the coconut milk slowly, about 1/2 cup at a time, and continue stirring and adding more as it is absorbed. Once the rice is tender and most of the liquid has been absorbed, about 30 minutes more (the rice will still look somewhat soupy), add the cream, if desired, and cook for another minute.

Remove the rice from the heat, remove and discard the vanilla bean pod, and set the pudding aside to cool slightly. Stir in the lime zest, if desired.

The pudding can be served immediately, or it can be refrigerated for up to 4 days in an airtight container.

# SPICED MINTY TAPIOCA

**SERVES 4 /** As a kid, I ate tapioca a lot, and I have always loved its interesting texture, with the surprise of tiny chewy nuggets. Now I see that my childhood favorite is also a great carrier for other subtle flavors. This version is lighter than the puddings I remember because it is made without eggs and with refreshing mint and spices. It is best served warm but is good cold as well.

5 1/4 CUPS WHOLE MILK

3/4 CUP SUGAR

1/2 TEASPOON SALT

1/2 VANILLA BEAN, SPLIT LENGTHWISE, OR SUBSTITUTE 1/2 TEASPOON PURE VANILLA EXTRACT

4 WHOLE STAR ANISE

1 CINNAMON STICK

8 SPRIGS MINT

3 STRIPS LEMON ZEST, ABOUT 2 INCHES BY 3/4 INCH (USE A VEGETABLE PEELER)

1 CUP SMALL PEARL TAPIOCA

In a medium saucepan over medium-high heat, combine 5 cups of the milk, the sugar, and salt. Scrape the seeds from the vanilla bean into the milk, and add the pod. Add the star anise, cinnamon stick, 4 of the mint sprigs, and lemon zest. When the milk begins to simmer, decrease the heat to low and simmer for 20 to 30 minutes. Remove from the heat and let the mixture steep for another 20 to 30 minutes (or refrigerate the milk mixture up to 8 hours or overnight, to intensify the flavors).

Strain the milk, discard the solids, and return the milk to the saucepan over medium-high heat. When the milk begins to simmer, add the tapioca. Decrease the heat to medium-low and simmer, stirring frequently, until the tapioca pearls have swelled and most of the liquid has been absorbed, 40 to 50 minutes. The mixture will be somewhat soupy, like a risotto, and will thicken as it sits or when it is refrigerated.

To serve, divide the pudding among 4 bowls and garnish with the remaining mint sprigs. It can be refrigerated, covered tightly with plastic wrap, for up to 3 days. To serve after refrigerating, put it in a medium saucepan over medium heat and stir in 1/4 cup milk, or more if needed, to help soften the tapioca to its original consistency as it heats.

**NOTE**

The pudding can be made with skim or low-fat milk, but it will not taste as rich and creamy.

# BITTERSWEET CHOCOLATE AND CHERRY PUDDING

*SERVES 6 /* This is the way chocolate pudding was meant to be—you can't beat the luxurious flavor of excellent chocolate and the creamy richness of the custard base. Sour cherries add a bit of surprise. | Fresh cherries might make the pudding watery, but rehydrated dried fruit adds exactly the right texture.

1/2 CUP DRIED SOUR CHERRIES
  (SEE SOURCES)

1 CUP SUGAR

2 TABLESPOONS CORNSTARCH

PINCH OF SALT

2 2/3 CUPS WHOLE MILK

3 EGG YOLKS

8 OUNCES GOOD-QUALITY BITTERSWEET
  OR SEMISWEET CHOCOLATE, SUCH
  AS CALLEBAUT (SEE SOURCES),
  COARSELY CHOPPED

1 TABLESPOON BUTTER

3/4 TEASPOON PURE VANILLA EXTRACT

Put the cherries in a bowl, add hot water to cover, and set them aside to soften for about 20 minutes. Drain well.

In a medium, heavy saucepan, off heat, whisk together the sugar, cornstarch, and salt. In a medium bowl, whisk together the milk and egg yolks, then gradually pour the mixture into the saucepan, whisking to combine. Add the chopped chocolate. Place the saucepan over medium heat, bring to a boil, and boil for 2 to 3 minutes, whisking continuously to melt the chocolate. Remove the pan from the heat and whisk in the butter, vanilla, and cherries. The pudding will be a little soupy, but it will become firmer once it has cooled in the refrigerator.

Divide the pudding among six 4- to 6-ounce ramekins or small bowls. Cover with plastic wrap and refrigerate for 3 to 8 hours, until set. It can be refrigerated for up to 3 days.

VARIATION

Make the pudding without the cherries, or substitute 1/2 cup toasted nuts for the cherries.

# GIANDUJA PUDDING

SERVES 6 / Made with gianduja, a hazelnut-flavored chocolate, this is an elegant version of the Bittersweet Chocolate and Cherry Pudding (page 165). If you like the combination of hazelnuts and chocolate, this may become your favorite dessert. | Gianduja can be challenging to find, but it is worth the effort. Like so many fine ingredients, it can be ordered online.

1/2 CUP SUGAR

2 TABLESPOONS CORNSTARCH

PINCH OF SALT

2 2/3 CUPS WHOLE MILK

3 EGG YOLKS

8 OUNCES GIANDUJA CHOCOLATE
    (SEE SOURCES), COARSELY CHOPPED

1 TABLESPOON BUTTER

1/2 PINT RASPBERRIES (OPTIONAL)

1/2 CUP CHOPPED TOASTED HAZELNUTS
    (PAGE 18; OPTIONAL)

In a medium, heavy saucepan, off heat, whisk together the sugar, cornstarch, and salt. In a medium bowl, whisk together the milk and egg yolks, and gradually pour the mixture into the saucepan, whisking to combine. Add the chopped chocolate. Place the saucepan over medium heat, bring to a boil, and boil for 1 minute, whisking continuously to melt the chocolate. Remove the pan from the heat and whisk in the butter. The pudding will be somewhat soupy, but it will become firm once it has fully cooled in the refrigerator.

Divide the pudding among six 4- to 6-ounce ramekins or small bowls. Cover with plastic wrap and chill in the refrigerator for 3 to 8 hours, until set. The pudding can be refrigerated for up to 3 days.

Serve as is, or top with a few raspberries or chopped hazelnuts, if desired.

# MENUS

The menus in this chapter will enhance your planning for all sorts of get-togethers, from a simple weekend lunch to a festive dinner party to a child-friendly meal. The combinations of dishes are meant as suggestions and are by no means written in stone. Use them as starting points for your own imaginative pairings. And feel free to add a touch of green—your favorite salad or sautéed fresh vegetables—at will.

### SATURDAY LUNCH AT HOME
ARUGULA WITH MANCHEGO, ROASTED ALMONDS, AND
   QUINCE DRESSING
SEARED TUNA WITH GINGER DRESSING
CARAMELIZED MANGO WITH LIME AND BLUEBERRIES

### DAZZLING DINNER PARTY
SUGAR-CURED SALMON WITH RICOTTA TOASTS
ZUCCHINI CARPACCIO WITH BLACK TRUFFLE AND OLIVE OIL
HAZELNUT-CRUSTED FOIE GRAS WITH FENNEL AND
   POMEGRANATE
SAUTÉED LOBSTER WITH ASPARAGUS AND BLOOD ORANGES
PINEAPPLE AND RHUBARB WITH BROWN SUGAR AND BASIL

### COMFORT FOOD
SWEET PEA SOUP WITH BASIL AND ALMOND PESTO
TRUFFLED MACARONI AND CHEESE
CHOCOLATE GANACHE CAKE WITH WHIPPED CREAM

### TURN UP THE THERMOSTAT
CAULIFLOWER SOUP WITH GREEN APPLE AND FROMAGE
   BLANC
CREAMY TAGLIATELLE WITH ROASTED RADICCHIO AND
   SHAVED ASIAGO
WARM ARBORIO RICE PUDDING WITH VANILLA AND
   COCONUT

### BRING THE KIDS
BLT PIZZA
CHEDDAR MEATLOAF
FIVE-SPICE SQUASH PURÉE
BITTERSWEET CHOCOLATE AND CHERRY PUDDING

### TOTALLY VEGETARIAN
SASHIMI OF AVOCADO WITH LIME AND ALMOND OIL
PORTOBELLO PICCATA WITH ALMOND BREAD CRUMBS,
   ROSEMARY, AND BALSAMIC VINAIGRETTE
BANANA CAKE

### AUTUMN DINNER
PAN-CRISPED GOAT CHEESE WITH FIGS AND ARUGULA
OSSO BUCO WITH DRIED ORANGE, THYME, AND WHITE
   BEANS
BRAISED AND CARAMELIZED FENNEL
RIPE PERSIMMONS WITH MINT SYRUP

### A MEDITERRANEAN MEAL
LIME AND HONEY GLAZED EGGPLANT WITH MINT CHUTNEY
DUCK BREAST WITH POMEGRANATE BASTE
COUSCOUS WITH TOASTED ALMONDS AND CUMIN
AMARETTO MILK-SOAKED CAKE

**CHRISTMAS/HOLIDAY FEAST**

CARPACCIO OF CÈPES WITH WISCONSIN ASIAGO AND
  BALSAMIC SYRUP

SEARED SCALLOPS WITH CARAMELIZED CAULIFLOWER AND
  BROWN BUTTER VINAIGRETTE

ROAST CHICKEN WITH LEMON, SAGE, AND PINE NUTS

BRAISED AND CARAMELIZED FENNEL

POLENTA WITH GOAT CHEESE AND ROSEMARY

GIANDUJA PUDDING


**AFTERNOON AT THE BEACH HOUSE**

MOROCCAN SPICED SHRIMP WITH ARTICHOKES AND
  POMEGRANATE

CHARRED VEGETABLES WITH ORANGE BLOSSOM HONEY
  AND PECORINO

RED CHILE BARBECUED SALMON WITH COCONUT
  BASMATI RICE

BITTERSWEET CHOCOLATE BRUSCHETTA


**STOP BY AFTER WORK**

RAW MUSHROOM SALAD WITH FENNEL AND PARMESAN

CHICKEN GLAZED WITH HONEY, LIME, AND CHILE

COUSCOUS WITH TOASTED ALMONDS AND CUMIN

STRAWBERRIES WITH POMEGRANATE MOLASSES AND
  FRESH RICOTTA

# INDEX

# TABLE OF EQUIVALENTS

The exact equivalents in the following tables have been rounded for convenience.

## LIQUID/DRY MEASURES

| U.S. | METRIC |
|---|---|
| 1/4 teaspoon | 1.25 milliliters |
| 1/2 teaspoon | 2.5 milliliters |
| 1 teaspoon | 5 milliliters |
| 1 tablespoon (3 teaspoons) | 15 milliliters |
| 1 fluid ounce (2 tablespoons) | 30 milliliters |
| 1/4 cup | 60 milliliters |
| 1/3 cup | 80 milliliters |
| 1/2 cup | 120 milliliters |
| 1 cup | 240 milliliters |
| 1 pint (2 cups) | 480 milliliters |
| 1 quart (4 cups, 32 ounces) | 960 milliliters |
| 1 gallon (4 quarts) | 3.84 liters |
| 1 ounce (by weight) | 28 grams |
| 1 pound | 454 grams |
| 2.2 pounds | 1 kilogram |

## LENGTH

| U.S. | METRIC |
|---|---|
| 1/8 inch | 3 millimeters |
| 1/4 inch | 6 millimeters |
| 1/2 inch | 12 millimeters |
| 1 inch | 2.5 centimeters |

## OVEN TEMPERATURE

| FAHRENHEIT | CELSIUS | GAS |
|---|---|---|
| 250 | 120 | 1/2 |
| 275 | 140 | 1 |
| 300 | 150 | 2 |
| 325 | 160 | 3 |
| 350 | 180 | 4 |
| 375 | 190 | 5 |
| 400 | 200 | 6 |
| 425 | 220 | 7 |
| 450 | 230 | 8 |
| 475 | 240 | 9 |
| 500 | 260 | 10 |